THE **PRESSURE COOKER** COOKBOOK

THE **PRESSURE COOKER** COOKBOOK

GINA STEER

CONTEMPORARY BOOKS

A QUINTET BOOK

This book was designed and produced by
Quintet Publishing Limited
6 Blundell Street
London N7 9BH

Senior Project Editor: Toria Leitch
Editor: Anna Bennett
Designer: Deep Design
Photographer: Ferguson Hill
Food Stylist: Vicki Smallwood
Creative Director: Richard Dewing

Typeset in Great Britain by Central Southern
Typesetters, Eastbourne
Manufactured in Hong Kong by Regent Publishing
Services Limited

Published by Contemporary Books
A division of NTC/Contemporary Publishing Group, Inc.
4255 West Touhy Avenue, Lincolnwood (Chicago), Illinois
60712-1975 U.S.A.

Printed in China by Leefung-Asco Printers Trading Limited
International Stardard Book Number: 0-8092-9476-1
01 02 03 04 05   15 14 13 12 11 10 9 8 7 6 5 4 3 2 1

Library of Congress Cataloging-in-Publication Data
Steer, Gina.
    The pressure cooker cookbook: 100 contemporary recipes for the time-pressured cook/
Gina Steer.
        p. cm.
    Originally published: London, UK : Quintet Pub., 2001.
    ISBN 0-8092-9476-1
        I. Pressure cookery. I. Title.

TX840.P7 S74 2001
641.5'87—dc21
                                                    00-52607

AUTHOR'S ACKNOWLEDGMENTS

An enormous thanks to Juliet Barker, who has done a fantastic job in helping me test the recipes ensuring that
they all work well. Thanks also to Vicki Smallwood who has toiled so hard in a hot photographic studio to
produce such stunning pictures with photographer Ferguson Hill.

I would like to thank Prestige for their help while writing this book, and for the loan of pressure cookers for both
testing and photography of the recipes. Also to Divertimenti for the loan of a pressure cooker.

CONTENTS

INTRODUCTION **6**

INDEX **128**

 17 BROTHS AND SOUPS

 31 FISH

 45 MEAT

 67 POULTRY

 89 VEGETABLES

 103 DRIED BEANS, PASTA, AND CEREALS

 117 DESSERTS AND PRESERVES

INTRODUCTION

I have a vivid childhood memory of the steam and hissing coming from the pressure cooker as my mother cooked all manner of dishes and, of course, the inevitable occasional accident when our dinner, be it soup or casserole, ended up on the ceiling, much to my amusement and my mother's annoyance.

Time moves on, however, and pressure cookers are now state-of-the-art, stylish pieces of equipment, far safer and easier to use, and well suited to the twenty-first century lifestyle. Pressure cooking is healthy due to the minimal amount of fat used, which helps to reduce cholesterol levels. It is also quick. We are all living life on the edge with very little spare time and often find it difficult to cook a healthy, nutritious, and delicious meal for our family and friends. A pressure cooker can provide such a meal in minutes so the pressure is on the pressure cooker rather than us.

If you are a newcomer to this method of cooking, I am confident that with a little practice you will not be able to imagine life without it. So welcome to the world of pressure cooking, which will give you twice the flavor in less than half the time.

PRESSURE COOKER BASICS

Before you start cooking with your pressure cooker there are a few imperative guidelines to bear in mind. There is a wide range of pressure cookers available and it is important that you read the manufacturer's instructions carefully before using yours for the first time because directions can vary from one model to another.

The principle behind pressure cooking is that ingredients and liquid are enclosed in the cooker and the steam, which in a normal saucepan is allowed to escape freely, is controlled, thus increasing the pressure and cooking temperature. It is this high temperature as well as the steam being forced through the food that cooks the food quickly and tenderizes it at the same time. Under normal conditions water boils at 212°F; this is dictated by atmospheric pressure and cannot be increased however long the water boils. The cook control on the pressure cooker increases the pressure inside the cooker, which in turn raises the temperature at which the liquid boils, thus leading to the rapid cooking time.

With most cookers the prepared food is put into the cooker with the required amount of liquid. The amount of liquid is important because the pressure cooker must not boil dry while under pressure, so there should always be at least 1¼ cups in the cooker. The lid is then closed and fixed into position and the cooker placed over the heat and brought quickly to pressure. Then the heat is reduced slightly and the cooking time should then be timed.

GENERAL RULES FOR PRESSURE COOKING

- Never leave your pressure cooker unattended on a hot stove. This could result in the cooker boiling dry and will cause damage. If this should happen, switch off the heat and allow the cooker to cool before moving.

- Add sufficient liquid to the cooker. You will need at least 1¼ cups of liquid to cover the first 15 minutes of cooking time then a further ¾ cup of liquid for every additional 15 minutes of cooking time.

- Never overfill your cooker and remember that different foods require different filling levels. With cereals, dried beans, and lentils, for example, the cooker must be no more than one-third full including the liquid.

- With soups, rice, pasta, and some stews the cooker should be no more than half-full including the liquid. Solid foods such as joints, vegetables, and one-pot meals should be no more than two-thirds full.

- Ensure that your stove is suitable for your pressure cooker. The base of the pressure cooker should sit comfortably on the heat source and be of a similar size.

- If using gas make sure that the flames do not go up the sides of the pressure cooker.

- If using containers to cook inside the pressure cooker, make sure they are ovenproof and fit well. They need to be able to withstand a temperature of 262°F.

- Do not place containers on top of foods that swell during cooking such as rice, dried beans, cereals, and pasta.

- When steaming, secure the waxed paper firmly. I have found that waxed paper is better than foil when steaming.

- Do not use metal or plastic in the cooker.

- Lightly oil your trivet when placing items of food on it to prevent sticking.

- If cooking dumplings, do not cook under pressure—otherwise the dumpling mixture may block the safety outlet on rising. Add the dumplings once the cooker has depressurized and do not close the lid.

- Finally, take care not to damage the various parts of the cooker because this will affect the efficiency of the cooker.

YOUR PRESSURE COOKER

When deciding what size of pressure cooker to buy, it is important that you consider your lifestyle. A 9-pint cooker is sufficient as you become familiar with using a pressure cooker; a smaller cooker would be useful for cooking rices and grains while a larger cooker is ideal for broth, or cooking in large quantities. Modern pressure cookers have back-up mechanisms, which prevent the build up of excess pressure thus making the cookers far safer to use than earlier models. All will have the same features although these may be called by different names.

Modern cookers have a *rise and time indicator*. This is a small round plug that rises and indicates that the pressure cooker has reached and is maintaining the correct internal temperature. If it should fall down while cooking under pressure, most probably it is because the heat is too low on the base, so increase the heat slightly. The cookers also have a *ready to serve indicator* which is a rubber plug and pintle. This tells you what is happening inside the pressure cooker; the indicator rises when the cooker is sealed and drops down once the pressure has been released, thus allowing the lid to be released. Ensure at all times that the rise and time indicator and ready to serve indicator are kept clean and free from food particles. Clean gently with a soft brush and soapy water. Check the manufacturer's instructions.

Some cookers have two *cook controls*, some three, each a different weight. The weight that is used the most is the heaviest, 15 lb, which works for most foods. The 10-lb cook control is used for preserves and delicate foods and is often used for steaming puddings. When using the 10-lb cook control, the rise and time indicator does not rise and the timing is carried out when there is a gentle hissing and escape of steam from around the weight. If the heat setting is too high, a loud hissing will occur. Lower the base heat. If no hissing is heard, increase the base heat, as the setting is too low and the food will not cook.

If a 5 lb cook control is provided this should be used for delicate foods as above.

Inside your cooker you will find a *separator*, which is a small basket ideal for cooking one-pot meals or small puddings or fish. If used for rice or pasta, line with foil. It is also useful for cooking different vegetables at the same time, as the separator can be sectioned with the dividers that sit inside the basket.

The *trivet* sits inside the cooker, rim-side down, often to place food on or to divide different types of food.

A rubber seal or *gasket* fits inside the lid and is vital to ensure that the cooker seals properly. It is important that the gasket is kept clean and it is a good idea to clean after each use and allow the gasket to dry naturally before refitting.

After cooking, remove the food as soon as possible from the cooker. Do not leave food in for long periods because this may cause staining. Wash in hot soapy water, rinse thoroughly, and dry after each use. If any food sticks, either soak the cooker in soapy water for a short period or use a plastic scrubbing brush or steel wool. Do not use bleach because this will cause staining.

If any food has actually burnt on, make up a strong solution using cream of tartar and water, bring to a boil, then simmer for about 20 minutes. Discard water and wash in soapy water, rinse, and dry.

Add a little lemon juice to the water in the cooker when steaming to prevent discoloration.

If you use the cooker regularly, the gasket and ready to serve indicator will need to be changed about every 6 months.

TROUBLESHOOTING

- **Cooker will not come to pressure**—the ready to serve indicator or the lid gasket may be leaking. Lightly oil the gasket and if this does not work, replace the faulty part.

- **Lid gasket leaks**—the rim of cooker is dirty. Wash the gasket and cooker rim. If this does not work, check if the gasket is worn and replace if necessary. Check whether the body or lid of the cooker is damaged and if so return to manufacturer and ensure that the correct gasket is fitted.

- **Excess steam for cook control**—this could mean that the heat is too high, the weight is not fitted correctly, or the weight support is loose. Either reduce the heat, or click the weight into place with a thick cloth or oven gloves and if the support is loose, cool the cooker, remove the weight and lid, and tighten the weight support.

- **Ready to serve indicator and pintle rises and ejects steam vertically**—the weight support is blocked and cannot vent correctly. Cool then clean the cook control support and reset the ready to serve indicator.

- **Ready to serve indicator blows out completely**—the weight support is blocked. Cool, clean the cook control support, and fit a new ready to serve indicator.

- **Cooker boils dry**—this is due to a couple of reasons: the lid gasket or the ready to serve indicator is leaking, in which case return to the manufacturer. This can also happen if you have been cooking on too high a heat for too long, or have used insufficient liquid for the cooking time.

TIPS AND TECHNIQUES

Cooking times vary with pressure cooking and times given can therefore only be a guide. When cooking vegetables, I have tried to undercook because it takes no time at all to return the cooker to pressure if necessary whereas once overcooked, vegetables cannot be recovered.

Ensure that the lid is locked firmly in place before you start to bring the cooker to pressure. Normally the lid will just slide and lock into the cooker. Many cookers have arrows or dots to indicate how to locate the lid. If the lid seems difficult to close, smear the inside of the rim of the lid with a little oil.

It can take from 30 seconds to 20 minutes to bring the food to pressure, depending on the food and quantity being cooked. To speed this time up use boiling, not cold, liquid.

Unless stated otherwise, the pressure cooking time commences once the pressure is reached. It is at this point that you should lower the heat and begin timing. If the pressure goes down, increase the heat slightly under the cooker as quickly as possible. It is important that the heat is lowered once pressure is reached, if not, the pressure will continue to rise, resulting in loud hissing sounds.

A heat diffuser is a good investment especially if your cooker is old. It also helps when cooking rice and dried beans, which may stick.

There are two ways of releasing the pressure: quickly (a method used for most foods) and depressurizing slowly (a method used for foods that may block up the vents such as rice, jam, or milk puddings).

When using your cooker for steamed puddings it is important that a presteaming time is used. This is important to ensure that the rising agent will be able to work. Without this the puddings will be heavy and stodgy.

Check your manufacturer's handbook on how to presteam. Remember that these puddings are cooked under 10 lb cook control and the rise and time indicator will not rise during the cooking process.

HINTS FOR COOKING
PASTA, RICE, AND CEREALS

- Rice, pasta, and cereals can be cooked in the base of the cooker as well as in the separator or a solid container. If cooking in the perforated separator, line with aluminum foil before cooking.

- Do not fill the cooker more than half-full and bring to pressure over a medium heat.

- Keep the heat slightly lower than usual to prevent the contents from frothing up and blocking any vents.

- Depressurize slowly.

- If using a container, ensure that it will fit inside the cooker then, if necessary, line with foil, place 8 oz pasta or rice into the container, pour in 2 cups boiling liquid then cover with waxed paper and secure.

- Use 15 lb cook control unless otherwise stated and depressurize slowly after cooking.

- When cooking pot barley or coarse oatmeal make sure that the cooker is not more than half-full and use 3¾ cups of boiling water for every 4 oz of grain. Bring to a boil over a medium heat and cook on a lower heat setting.

- Bulgur wheat and millet should be cooked in an ovenproof container or foil-lined separator, not in the body of the cooker. Depressurize slowly.

- When cooking rice with milk for puddings, only use 2½ cups milk to 2 oz rice. Bring the milk to a boil in the open cooker, add the rice and stir until it comes back to a boil. Lower the heat to a rolling boil, then close the lid, and bring to 15-lb pressure. Depressurize slowly.

COOKING TIMES

REMEMBER TO USE THE CORRECT AMOUNT OF LIQUID WHEN COOKING. THESE REQUIRE SLOW DEPRESSURIZING.

PASTA, RICE, AND CEREALS

Variety	Cooking time
¼ cup pot barley	20 minutes
1 cup coarse oatmeal	15 minutes
1 cup long-grain rice	2 minutes
1¼ cups brown rice	3 minutes
8 oz spaghettini	2 minutes
8 oz spaghetti/tagliatelle	3 minutes

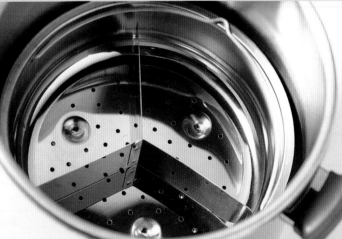

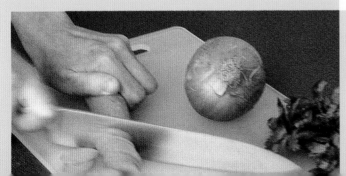

HINTS FOR **COOKING BEANS**

- With all dried beans it is very important to soak them in boiling water for at least 1 hour before cooking. Drain the beans and place in the cooker and do not fill the cooker more than one-third full after both the beans and liquid have been added.

- Add 2½ cups of fresh water or broth for every cup of dried beans (this weight is before soaking).

- Do not add salt to the cooker when cooking beans as this toughens the beans. Season once the beans are done.

- Bring to a boil, remove any scum that floats to the surface, then reduce the heat so that the liquid is gently simmering before closing the lid. Bring to pressure at this simmering heat.

- Always depressurize slowly at the end of cooking time or the vents may become blocked.

- Use 15 lb cook control unless the recipe specifies otherwise.

- If cooking different varieties together, check they all have the same cooking times.

COOKING TIMES

REMEMBER TO USE THE CORRECT AMOUNT OF LIQUID WHEN COOKING. THESE REQUIRE SLOW DEPRESSURIZING.

BEANS, PEAS, AND LENTILS

Variety	Cooking time
Aduki	5 minutes
Black beans	10 minutes
Black-eyed peas	10 minutes
Borlotti beans	10 minutes
Cannellini beans	10 minutes
Flageolet beans	5 minutes
Garbanzos	20 minutes
Lentils—brown	3 minutes
Lentils—green	3 minutes
Lentils—red, no soak	Just bring to pressure
Lima beans	15 minutes
Mung beans	Just bring to pressure
Navy beans—large	15 minutes
Navy beans—small	10 minutes
Peas—marrowfat	20 minutes
Peas—split	3 minutes
Peas—whole	5 minutes
Pinto beans	12 minutes
Red kidney beans	10 minutes
Soy beans	25 minutes

GUIDELINES FOR
MEAT AND POULTRY

ALL TIMES ARE FOR POT ROASTING PER 1 LB—USE 15 LB COOK CONTROL.
REFER TO MANUFACTURER'S INSTRUCTIONS.

- Pork and poultry should always be defrosted before cooking.

- When making casseroles do not coat in seasoned flour but thicken at the end of cooking. This applies to all foods.

- When cooking meat from frozen, cut into smaller pieces before freezing then place in the open cooker and brown, keeping the heat lower than usual to prevent spitting. Add about 5 minutes to the cooking time or if a joint allow an extra 10 minutes per pound.

- It is possible to reheat frozen cooked casseroles. Do not use the trivet and add 1¼ cups of liquid to the frozen food. Cook for 8 to 10 minutes depending on meat size. Depressurize quickly then adjust the consistency of the sauce.

- Joints should be no larger than 3 lb. Do not fill the cooker more than half-full when all the vegetables and liquid have been added.

- Prepare whole birds by washing thoroughly inside the cavity and truss smaller birds to make them easier to handle. Cut large birds into portions so that the steam can circulate freely.

COOKING TIMES

JOINT	FROM DEFROSTED	FROM FROZEN
Beef		
Topside	12 minutes	22 minutes
Brisket	30 minutes	30 minutes
Pot roast joints	15 minutes	25 minutes
Lamb		
Boned and rolled breast	15 minutes	25 minutes
Boned and rolled shoulder	15 minutes	25 minutes
Neck	12 minutes	22 minutes
Pork		
Boned and rolled shoulder	15 minutes	do not cook
Loin	12 minutes	from frozen
BOILING		
Bacon	8 minutes	do not cook from frozen
Brisket	20 minutes	30 minutes

GUIDELINES FOR **FISH**

- Remove the fins, scales, and if necessary clean whole fish then rinse thoroughly.

- Cook in the cooker with a minimum of 1¼ cups cooking liquid. If using milk, cook on a medium setting then use the milk to make the accompanying sauce.

- Oil the trivet thoroughly before use and place the fish on top. The fish can be placed on a sheet of waxed paper or foil for ease of handling.

- Fish needs only a short cooking time, so time carefully and depressurize quickly unless cooking with milk, in which case the pressure should be released slowly.

- If cooking fish from frozen add an extra 1 minute if the fish is whole or a thick steak, and add an extra 2 minutes if cooking by weight.

- For all white fish, such as haddock, cod, or halibut—
    cook fillets for 3 to 4 minutes
    cook steaks 4 to 5 minutes
  This also includes hake, herring, salmon, trout, mackerel, and turbot fillets. More delicate fish, such as sole and flounder fillets, take 3 minutes. Whole fish take around 5 to 7 minutes, depending on size.

GUIDELINES FOR **STEAMED PUDDINGS, DESSERTS, AND PRESERVES**

The pressure cooker is ideal for cooking all types of steamed puddings, desserts, and preserves. There are just a few guidelines to remember to ensure a perfect result every time.

- Any container used must be ovenproof and filled no more than two-thirds full.

- Ensure you oil the container well and place a small circle of waxed paper in the base. Cover with a double sheet of waxed paper with a pleat in the center or a single sheet of foil and secure firmly.

- Pour 4 cups boiling water into the cooker with 2 tablespoons of lemon juice to prevent discoloration.

- All puddings must be presteamed first in order to make the rising agent work. See individual recipes and refer to manufacturer's handbook.

- Depressurize slowly so the pudding does not collapse and sink.

- Milk puddings can be cooked in a pressure cooker, but make sure the heat is not too hot on the base or they can burn.

- Christmas or Plum Puddings can be cooked in the pressure cooker. Refer to manufacturer's instructions for specific cooking times.

- Preserves can be cooked in a much shorter time than with conventional cooking. The fruit is softened in the cooker under pressure then once the sugar is added, the preserve is cooked without the lid. Refer to manufacturer's instructions for specific times. The same general guidelines apply to preserves whether cooked in a pressure cooker or in a conventional manner.

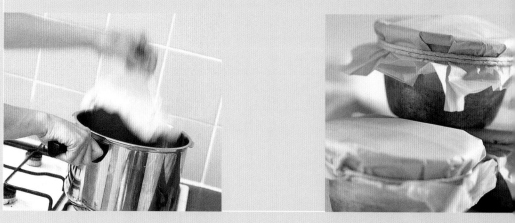

GUIDELINES FOR **VEGETABLES** **COOKING TIMES**

Vegetables require very little cooking time in the pressure cooker, especially if you prefer not to overcook them. Some, such as asparagus, green beans, and cabbage, are best steamed or cooked in a conventional pan.

- If you do cook green vegetables in a pressure cooker, however, add them to boiling water. Use the 15-lb cook control and depressurize quickly.

- Save time and fuel by cooking a selection of vegetables together. Cut them into even-size pieces, and use the separator and dividers.

- If liked, cook root vegetables on the trivet with 1¼ cups water, bring to a boil, then place green vegetables in the separator, place on top of the trivet, close the lid, and bring to pressure. Depressurize quickly.

How long you cook your vegetables is a matter of choice. The table listed here will give you crisp rather than well-cooked vegetables. If you like softer vegetables, just increase the cooking time slightly. Bear in mind that root vegetables need to be properly cooked.

REMEMBER TO USE THE CORRECT AMOUNT OF LIQUID WHEN COOKING. THESE REQUIRE SLOW DEPRESSURIZING.

Variety	Cooking time
Asparagus—tied into small bundles	2 to 4 minutes, depending on age
Artichokes	6 to 8 minutes, depending on size
Artichokes—Jerusalem	4 to 5 minutes
Beans—fava, French, green	1 to 3 minutes depending on age
Beets	Do not peel and leave a small amount of stalk and root. Wash carefully and cook for 2 to 4 minutes
Broccoli	1 to 2 minutes
Cabbage—shredded	Just bring to pressure
Cabbage—red	3 minutes
Carrots	3 to 4 minutes
Cauliflower—florets	1 to 2 minutes
Celery—cut into short lengths	2 minutes
Corn on the cob	6 to 10 minutes, depending on size
Eggplant	2 to 4 minutes depending on size
Fennel	2 to 4 minutes, depending if halved or sliced
Leeks, sliced	2 to 3 minutes
Okra	2 to 3 minutes
Onions—whole	3 to 4 minutes
Parsnips—sliced or halved	3 to 4 minutes
Potatoes—new, whole	4 minutes
Potatoes—cut into chunks	4 minutes
Rutabaga and yams	6 minutes
Spinach	Just bring to pressure, with a little water
Sweet potatoes—sliced	4 to 5 minutes
Winter squash	6 to 10 minutes depending on type and quantity
Turnips	3 to 4 minutes
Zucchini—cut into thick slices	Just bring to pressure

ADAPTING OTHER RECIPES

It is very easy to adapt your own recipes once you have become used to pressure cooking. First of all refer to the manufacturer's cookbook for a similar recipe to the timings and method of depressurizing and remember that pressure cooking time is usually about two-thirds less than normal cooking.

Use liquids that produce steam, such as broth, wine, or milk. Do not use melted butter or oil except to brown foods first and ensure that you use the minimal amount.

An important note to remember is that the cooking time is determined by the size of the food, not the quantity. Joints of meat, on the other hand, are timed by weight.

Use a medium setting for rice, pasta, cereals, dried beans, beets, and milk or any other foods that will froth up during cooking.

For stews and casseroles, brown the meat in the open cooker first, then wipe the cooker clean afterward so the food does not burn when under pressure.

Some foods such as cook-in sauces and commercial soups may stick on the base so add an extra $^2/_3$ cup of liquid.

Never thicken stews, casseroles, soups, or any sauces before cooking under pressure, always afterward. This can be done either with cornstarch, beurre manié (a flour-and-butter paste) or mashed vegetables such as potatoes.

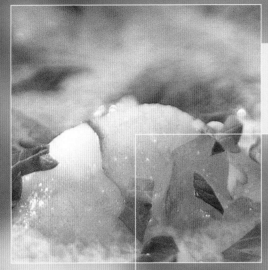

BROTHS
AND SOUPS

MEXICAN PINTO BEAN SOUP

IT IS IMPORTANT TO COVER THE DRIED BEANS WITH BOILING WATER AND SOAK FOR 1 HOUR BEFORE PROCEEDING. COOKING BEANS IN THE PRESSURE COOKER ENSURES THAT ALL TOXINS ARE DESTROYED.

Place the beans in a large bowl, cover with boiling water, and leave for at least 1 hour. Drain then place in the cooker and add 2¹/₂ cups of water. Bring to a boil and remove any scum from the surface. Reduce the heat to a rolling boil and cover with the lid then bring to 15 lb pressure.

Cook for 8 minutes then depressurize slowly. Remove the lid, lift out the beans from the cooker, and reserve. Rinse and dry the cooker.

Heat the oil in the open cooker and sauté the chile, garlic, and onion for 5 minutes.

Add the contents of the can of tomatoes with the broth, oregano, seasoning to taste, the lime zest and juice, and the reserved beans. Bring quickly back to a boil, cover with the lid, and bring to 15 lb pressure. Cook for 4 minutes.

Depressurize slowly, stir in the chopped cilantro, and adjust the seasoning to taste. Mix the chopped tomatoes and avocado together. Ladle the soup into individual serving bowls, add a spoonful of the sour cream and place a generous spoonful of the tomato and avocado on top.

Serves **6**
Cook control **15 lb**
Preparation time **15 minutes**
 plus 1 hour soaking time
Open cooking time **8 minutes**
Pressure cooking time **12 minutes**

1 cup dried pinto beans
2¹/₂ cups water
1 Tbsp olive oil
1 red chile seeded and chopped
4 garlic cloves, peeled
 and chopped
1 onion, peeled and chopped
One 14-oz can chopped tomatoes

2¹/₂ cups vegetable or chicken
 broth
1 Tbsp chopped fresh oregano
Salt and freshly ground
 black pepper
Grated zest and juice of 1 lime
2 Tbsp chopped fresh cilantro

TO SERVE

2 ripe tomatoes, peeled, seeded,
 and chopped
1 small ripe avocado, peeled,
 pitted, and diced fine
6 Tbsp sour cream

CHILLED WATERCRESS SOUP

THE SMALL AMOUNT OF CHILE IN THIS SOUP GIVES THIS CLASSIC SOUP A NEW TWIST.
THE PIQUANT FLAVOR IS DELICIOUS.

Wash the watercress, discarding any tough stalks, reserve a few sprigs for decoration, and chop the remainder.

Melt the butter in the open cooker and sauté the onion, garlic, potatoes, and crushed chiles for 5 minutes. Sprinkle in the flour and cook, stirring for 1 minute.

Add the broth, chopped watercress, and seasoning to taste, close the lid, and bring to 15 lb pressure. Cook for 4 minutes.

Depressurize quickly and adjust the seasoning. Cool slightly then purée in a food processor or blender. Allow to cool and stir in the sour cream. Chill then serve garnished with the reserved watercress sprigs.

Serves **6**
Cook control **15 lb**
Preparation time **5 minutes,**
   plus chilling time
Open cooking time **4 minutes**
Pressure cooking time **4 minutes**

8 oz watercress
2 Tbsp sweet butter
1 onion, peeled and chopped
1 to 2 garlic cloves, peeled and crushed

8 oz potatoes, peeled and diced
½ tsp dried crushed chiles
2 Tbsp white all-purpose flour
4 cups vegetable or chicken broth
Salt and freshly ground black pepper
⅔ cup sour cream

WILD MUSHROOM SOUP

ANY DRIED WILD MUSHROOMS WILL WORK WELL IN THIS RECIPE.
REMEMBER TO USE THE SOAKING LIQUID AS WELL FOR MAXIMUM FLAVOR.

Cover the dried mushrooms with almost-boiling water and soak for at least 20 minutes then drain, reserving the mushrooms and liquid.

Heat the oil in the open cooker and sauté the onions, garlic, chile, potato, and parsnip for 3 minutes, stirring frequently. Slice the mushrooms if large then add to the cooker and sauté for 1 minute. Add the broth, the rehydrated mushrooms with their soaking liquid, and bring to a boil.

Reduce the heat, close the lid, and bring to 15 lb pressure. Cook for 3 minutes then depressurize quickly and purée in batches in a blender.

Add seasoning to taste then reheat gently in the cleaned cooker before serving swirled with the cream or sour cream and sprinkled with the chives. Serve with warm crusty bread.

Serves **6**
Cook control **15 lb**
Preparation time **10 minutes,**
 plus 20 minutes soaking time
Open cooking time **5 minutes**
Pressure cooking time **3 minutes**

¼ oz/⅛ cup dried mushrooms
1 Tbsp oil
2 medium onions, peeled
 and chopped
3 to 5 garlic cloves, peeled
 and chopped
1 red jalapeño chile seeded
 and chopped fine
1 potato, about 8 oz in weight,
 peeled and chopped

1 medium parsnip, about 6 oz in
 weight, peeled and chopped
4½ cups assorted fresh
 mushrooms, such as
 chanterelle, oyster, morels,
 chestnut, and button
 mushrooms, wiped
4 cups vegetable broth
Salt and freshly ground
 black pepper

TO GARNISH
4 Tbsp light or sour cream and
 2 Tbsp snipped fresh chives

TO SERVE
Crusty bread

SHRIMP CHOWDER

CHOWDERS CAN BE MADE WITH A WIDE COMBINATION OF INGREDIENTS. THIS RECIPE IS
EXTRA SPECIAL BECAUSE IT USES JUMBO SHRIMP, SO IT IS IDEAL WHEN YOU ARE ENTERTAINING.

Serves **8**
Cook control **15 lb**
Preparation time **10 minutes**
Open cooking time **10 minutes**
Pressure cooking time **3 minutes**

8 oz raw jumbo shrimp
2 Tbsp sweet butter
8 slices bacon, chopped
1 onion, peeled and chopped
2 celery stalks, trimmed and chopped
8 oz potatoes, peeled and diced
1 bay leaf
3¾ cups fish or vegetable broth
3 Tbsp cornstarch
⅔ cup milk
4 oz peeled shrimp, defrosted if frozen
4 oz corn kernels, defrosted if frozen
Salt and freshly ground black pepper
2 to 3 Tbsp light cream
2 Tbsp chopped fresh parsley

Remove the heads from the jumbo shrimp and peel. Discard. Melt the butter in the open cooker and sauté the bacon, onion, and celery for 5 minutes. Add the potatoes and continue to sauté for a further 3 minutes. Add the bay leaf, broth, and jumbo shrimp.

Close the lid and bring to 15 lb pressure and cook for 3 minutes.

Depressurize quickly, stir, then remove the bay leaf. Blend the cornstarch with the milk and stir into the cooker. Stir over a gentle heat until the mixture comes to a boil. Add the remaining ingredients with seasoning to taste, simmer for 2 minutes, then serve with crusty granary bread.

CARROT AND LENTIL SOUP

FOR A CHANGE SUBSTITUTE 1¼ CUPS OF THE BROTH WITH ORANGE JUICE AND ADD 2 TABLESPOONS OF GRATED ORANGE ZEST BEFORE BRINGING TO PRESSURE. GARNISH WITH EXTRA ORANGE ZEST.

Serves **4**
Cook control **15 lb**
Preparation time **10 minutes**
Open cooking time **5 minutes**
Pressure cooking time **5 minutes**

1 Tbsp oil
1 medium onion, peeled and chopped
4 garlic cloves, peeled and chopped
1 lb carrots, peeled and chopped
¼ cup red split lentils
1 tsp ground cumin
1 tsp ground coriander

1 bay leaf
3¾ cups vegetable broth, heated to almost boiling
Salt and freshly ground black pepper
2 Tbsp chopped fresh cilantro
4 Tbsp low-fat, plain yogurt or light cream

TO SERVE
Crusty bread or croutons

Heat the oil in the open cooker and sauté the onion, garlic, and carrots for 3 minutes. Add the lentils, spices, and bay leaf and cook for 1 minute.

Pour in the hot broth and bring to a boil. Close the lid and bring to 15 lb pressure. Cook for 5 minutes. Depressurize slowly then discard the bay leaf.

Cool slightly then purée in the blender. Season to taste, add the chopped cilantro, and reheat gently.

Ladle into bowls and swirl a spoonful of yogurt or cream on top. Alternatively stir the yogurt or cream into the soup. Serve with crusty bread or croutons.

FISH BROTH

WHEN MAKING YOUR OWN BROTH IT IS VITAL THAT
ALL THE INGREDIENTS ARE EXTREMELY FRESH
OR THE FINISHED BROTH WILL BE IMPAIRED.

Makes about **2½ cups**	**1 cod's head or fish bones**
Cook control **15 lb**	**and trimmings**
Preparation time **4 minutes**	**1 celery stalk**
Open cooking time **3 minutes**	**2 bay leaves**
Pressure cooking time	**A few fresh parsley sprigs**
10 minutes	**A few fresh thyme sprigs**
	1 onion, peeled and sliced
	1 small carrot, peeled and sliced
	10 peppercorns
	Salt

Rinse the cod's head or bones and trimmings and place in the
open cooker. Cut the celery in half and place the bay leaves,
parsley, and thyme sprigs on one half of the celery and place
the second half on top. Tie securely and place in the cooker.
Add the onion, carrot, and peppercorns then pour in 5 cups
cold water.

Bring to a boil in the open cooker then remove any scum
which floats to the top with a slotted spoon. Add salt.

Close the lid and bring to 15 lb pressure. Cook for 10 minutes.
Depressurize slowly.

Strain, adjust the seasoning, and allow to cool. Use the same day.

If liked, the broth can be frozen once cool. Use half the amount
of liquid if freezing then add more water after defrosting.
Use within 3 months if frozen.

BEEF BROTH

IT IS AN EXCELLENT IDEA ONCE THE BROTH IS
MADE TO FREEZE SOME FOR LATER USE.
POUR INTO SMALL CONTAINERS OR ICE CUBE TRAYS
AND OPEN-FREEZE. ONCE FROZEN SOLID, PACK IN
HEAVY-DUTY FREEZER BAGS TO STORE. DO NOT
FORGET TO LABEL.

Makes about **2½ cups**	**2 lb meat bones, from either**
Cook control **15 lb**	**raw or cooked meat**
Preparation time **4 minutes**	**2 onions, peeled and chopped**
Open cooking time **3 minutes**	**2 carrots, peeled and chopped**
Pressure cooking time	**½ small head fennel, chopped**
15 minutes	**or 2 celery stalks, trimmed**
	and chopped
	10 peppercorns
	1 bouquet garni
	Salt

Wash the bones and chop into 3-inch lengths. Place in the open
cooker with 5 cups water and bring to a boil.

Remove any scum that floats to the surface with a slotted spoon.

Add the chopped vegetables with the peppercorns and bouquet
garni then bring to a boil, add salt, and close the lid.

Cook at 15 lb pressure and cook for 15 minutes. Depressurize
slowly then strain and skim off any fat from the surface.
Cool before using.

Once cool, cover and store in the refrigerator for up to 3 days.
Boil vigorously before use.

If using raw bones you can brown them in the open cooker
in a little oil first. Wipe the cooker clean before adding the
remaining ingredients.

CHICKEN BROTH

ANY POULTRY CARCASS CAN BE USED TO MAKE BROTH, BUT DO NOT USE DIFFERENT BIRDS AT THE SAME TIME. BREAK THE CARCASS UP INTO SMALLER PIECES SO THE BONES SIT EASILY IN THE COOKER.

Break the carcass into smaller pieces and place in the open cooker with any skin and pieces of chicken meat. Add the onion, carrot, and celery with the bay leaves and parsley. Add the cloves and peppercorns then pour in 5 cups cold water.

Bring to a boil and remove any scum that floats to the surface with a slotted spoon. Add salt.

Close the lid and bring to 15 lb pressure then cook for 10 minutes.

Depressurize slowly then strain, skim off any fat, and adjust the seasoning. Cool then use as required. If not using the same day, cool and store in the refrigerator for up to 3 days. Boil vigorously before use.

If freezing, use half the amount of liquid then add more water when defrosted.

Makes about **2½ cups**
Cook control **15 lb**
Preparation time **5 minutes**
Open cooking time **3 minutes**
Pressure cooking time **10 minutes**

Carcass of 1 cooked chicken
1 medium onion, peeled and sliced
1 medium carrot, peeled and sliced
2 celery stalks, trimmed and sliced
2 bay leaves
A few fresh parsley sprigs
2 whole cloves
A few whole white peppercorns
Salt

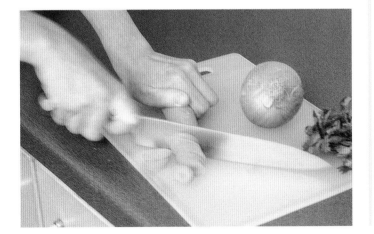

PESTO SOUP

PESTO HAS BECOME VERY POPULAR IN RECENT YEARS AND THIS SOUP TAKES THE IDEA A LITTLE FURTHER.
IF LIKED, SPRINKLE THE FINISHED SOUP WITH A FEW TOASTED PINE NUTS.

Trim the leeks, slice thin, and wash thoroughly. Heat the butter in the open cooker and sauté the leeks, garlic, and fennel for 5 minutes.

Add the remaining vegetables with the lemon zest, 2 tablespoons of the basil, broth, and seasoning. Close the lid and quickly bring to 15 lb pressure. Cook for 6 minutes then depressurize quickly.

Take out a little of the cooked vegetables then purée the remainder in a food processor or blender. Stir in the reserved vegetables and remaining basil. Heat gently then serve with the Parmesan cheese.

Serves **6**
Cook control **15 lb**
Preparation time **10 minutes**
Open cooking time **5 minutes**
Pressure cooking time **6 minutes**

3 leeks (about 12 oz)
2 Tbsp sweet butter
3 garlic cloves, peeled and crushed
1 head fennel, trimmed and chopped
2 zucchini, trimmed, sliced, and cut into
  half-moon shapes
4 oz green beans, trimmed and chopped
3 medium tomatoes, chopped and seeded
1 Tbsp grated lemon zest
3 Tbsp chopped fresh basil
4 cups vegetable or chicken broth
Salt and freshly ground black pepper

TO SERVE
Grated Parmesan cheese

BEAN GAZPACHO

YOU CAN ALSO SERVE THIS SOUP WARM. AFTER BLENDING, REHEAT GENTLY UNTIL PIPING HOT, THEN STIR IN THE CHOPPED GREEN BELL PEPPER, TOMATOES, CUCUMBER, VINEGAR, PARSLEY, AND SEASONING. HEAT THROUGH BRIEFLY THEN SERVE.

Serves **6**
Cook control **15 lb**
Preparation time **10 minutes**
  plus 1 hour soaking
Pressure cooking time
  10 minutes

1 cup dried cannellini beans
1 quart vegetable broth
4 to 6 garlic cloves, peeled
1 white onion, peeled
  and chopped
1 serrano chile, seeded and
  chopped

4 ripe but still firm tomatoes,
  seeded and chopped fine
One 2-inch piece cucumber,
  peeled, seeded and
  chopped fine
1 small green bell pepper,
  seeded and chopped fine
2 Tbsp sherry vinegar
Salt and freshly ground pepper
2 Tbsp freshly chopped flat-leaf
  parsley

TO SERVE
Croutons

Place the cannellini beans in a bowl and cover with boiling water and leave for 1 hour. Drain and place in the open cooker with 4 cups of the broth, garlic, onion, and chile. Bring to a boil then close the lid and bring to 15 lb pressure. Cook for 10 minutes then depressurize slowly.

Once cool purée in a blender if liked and chill.

When ready to serve, stir the chopped tomatoes, cucumber, green bell pepper, vinegar, seasoning to taste, and the chopped parsley. Serve with croutons.

BORSCHT

BORSCHT HAS THE MOST WONDERFUL DEEP PURPLE-RED COLOR. WITH THE ADDITION OF SOUR CREAM AND CHIVES A BOWL OF BORSCHT LOOKS AND TASTES ABSOLUTELY STUNNING.

Serves **4 to 6**
Cook control **15 lb**
Preparation time **10 minutes**
Open cooking time **3 minutes**
Pressure cooking time
  8 minutes

1½ lb raw beets, peeled
2 medium onions, peeled and
  chopped
2 garlic cloves, peeled and
  chopped

4 cups vegetable or beef broth
1¼ cups orange juice
5 to 6 Tbsp dry sherry
Salt and freshly ground black
  pepper

TO GARNISH
Half-fat crème fraîche or sour
  cream and fresh chives

TO SERVE
Sliced brown bread and butter
  or warm French bread

Grate or dice the beets and place in the open cooker with the onion, garlic, broth, and ⅔ cup of the orange juice then bring to a gentle boil. Close the lid and bring to 15 lb pressure and cook for 8 minutes.

Depressurize quickly then strain through a sieve and add the remaining orange juice, sherry, and seasoning to taste.

Either chill or reheat gently and serve in individual bowls topped with a spoonful of half-fat crème fraîche or sour cream and 2 chives arranged across the top. Serve with thinly sliced brown bread and butter if serving chilled or chunks of warm French bread if serving hot.

TOMATO AND GARBANZO SOUP

WHEN THE WEATHER BEGINS TO GET COOLER, SOUP IS ALWAYS POPULAR. THE SMALL AMOUNT OF CHILE WILL REMOVE ANY COLD-WEATHER CHILLS.

Place the garbanzos in a bowl and cover with boiling water, leave for 1 hour, then drain and place in the open cooker with 2½ cups water. Bring to a boil and remove any scum that rises to the surface with a slotted spoon. Reduce the heat to a gentle boil, close the lid, and bring to 15 lb pressure.

Cook for 15 minutes then depressurize slowly. Strain the garbanzos through a colander and reserve.

Rinse and dry the cooker.

Heat the oil in the open cooker and sauté the onion, chile, garlic, red bell pepper, and fennel for 3 minutes.

Add the chopped tomatoes with the oregano and the reserved garbanzos.

Blend the tomato paste with the broth and vinegar and pour into the cooker. Bring back to a boil then close the lid and bring to 15 lb pressure. Cook for 5 minutes then depressurize quickly and add seasoning to taste with the shredded basil.

Ladle into bowls and serve.

Serves **6**
Cook control **15 lb**
Preparation time **10 minutes plus**
  1 hour soaking time
Open cooking time **3 minutes**
Pressure cooking time **20 minutes**

¾ cup dried garbanzos
1 Tbsp oil
1 medium onion, peeled and chopped
1 jalapeño chile, seeded and chopped
3 garlic cloves, peeled and chopped
1 small red bell pepper, seeded and
  chopped
½ small head fennel, trimmed and
  chopped
12 oz ripe tomatoes, chopped
1 Tbsp chopped fresh oregano
2 Tbsp tomato paste
2½ cups vegetable broth
1 Tbsp red wine vinegar
Salt and freshly ground black pepper
2 Tbsp shredded basil

ROASTED BELL PEPPER SOUP

THE BELL PEPPERS CAN BE ROASTED EITHER IN THE OVEN OR UNDER A PREHEATED BROILER. ROASTING TAKES MUCH LONGER BUT GIVES A MORE INTENSE FLAVOR. CHARRING UNDER THE BROILER OR IN THE COOKER IS MUCH QUICKER.

Heat 2 teaspoons of the oil in the open cooker, add the bell peppers, and sauté for 8 minutes or until the skins have begun to char. Remove from the cooker with a slotted spoon, chop, and reserve. Wipe the pan clean.

Add the remaining oil with the garlic and onion and sauté for 3 minutes. Return the chopped bell peppers to the pan with the tomatoes, saffron, shredded basil, and broth. Add seasoning to taste and bring to a boil.

Close the lid and quickly bring to 15 lb pressure. Cook for 6 minutes then quickly depressurize.

Purée the soup in a blender, rub through a fine sieve, and adjust the seasoning. If serving warm, return to the rinsed cooker and heat gently. If serving cold, chill until required. Swirl with the cream or crème fraîche and serve garnished with the shredded basil and croutons.

Serves **6**
Cook control **15 lb**
Preparation time **10 minutes**
Open cooking time **11 minutes**
Pressure cooking time **6 minutes**

2 Tbsp olive oil
3 red bell peppers, seeded and quartered
3 garlic cloves, peeled and crushed
1 onion, peeled and chopped
1 lb large ripe tomatoes, chopped
A few strands saffron
1 Tbsp shredded basil leaves
4 cups vegetable or chicken broth
Salt and freshly ground black pepper
4 Tbsp light cream or half-fat crème fraîche

TO GARNISH
1 Tbsp shredded basil
Garlic croutons

POTATO AND SPINACH
VICHYSSOISE

THIS SOUP IS DELICIOUS SERVED EITHER WARM OR CHILLED. IF CHILLING, COOL AS QUICKLY AS POSSIBLE THEN CHILL IN THE REFRIGERATOR FOR AT LEAST 4 HOURS.

Serves **4 to 6**
Cook control **15 lb**
Preparation time **7 minutes**
Open cooking time **5 minutes**
Pressure cooking time **6 minutes**

1 Tbsp oil
1 medium onion, peeled and
  chopped
3 garlic cloves, peeled and
  chopped
10 oz potatoes, peeled and diced

1 large leek, about 8 oz in
  weight, trimmed and sliced
4 cups vegetable broth
2 Tbsp grated lemon zest
3 sprigs fresh dill
8 oz fresh spinach
Salt and freshly ground black
  pepper
⅔ cup light cream or rich milk

TO GARNISH
2 Tbsp chopped fresh dill

Heat the oil in the open cooker and sauté the onion, garlic, leek, and potatoes for 3 minutes. Add the broth, lemon zest, and dill sprigs and bring to a gentle boil.

Close the lid and bring to 15 lb pressure. Cook for 5 minutes then depressurize quickly.

Meanwhile discard any tough outer leaves and stems from the spinach, wash thoroughly, and chop. Open the cooker and add the spinach. Close the lid and return to pressure. Cook for 1 minute then depressurize quickly.

Purée in a blender, adjust the seasoning, then stir in the cream or milk. Reheat gently in the cleaned, open cooker for 2 minutes or until almost at boiling point, then serve sprinkled with the chopped dill

VEGETABLE BROTH

WHEN MAKING VEGETABLE BROTH DO NOT USE STARCHY FOODS OR GREEN VEGETABLES BECAUSE THEY WILL MAKE THE BROTH CLOUDY. IF LIKED, THE ONION SKINS CAN BE INCLUDED TO GIVE A DARKER BROTH. REMEMBER THAT ALL HOMEMADE BROTHS ARE AT THEIR BEST IF FRESHLY MADE. FREEZING LOSES A LITTLE OF THE FLAVOR.

Makes about **2½ cups**
Cook control **15 lb**
Preparation time **5 minutes**
Open cooking time **3 minutes**
Pressure cooking time
  10 minutes

2 onions, peeled and chopped
2 garlic cloves, peeled and
  chopped

1 large carrot, peeled and
  chopped
2 celery stalks, trimmed and
  chopped
1 small turnip, peeled and
  chopped
2 bay leaves
1 bouquet garni
5 peppercorns
Salt

Place the chopped vegetables in the open cooker with the bay leaves, bouquet garni, and peppercorns. Pour in 5 cups cold water and bring to a boil. Remove any scum that floats to the surface with a slotted spoon and then add salt.

Close the lid and bring to 15 lb pressure. Cook for 30 minutes. Depressurize quickly.

Strain the broth and allow to cool before using. Store in the refrigerator for up to 3 days. Boil vigorously before using.

If freezing, use half the quantity of water, freeze for up to 3 months, and once defrosted, add the remaining water.

FISH

SALMON WITH MUSHROOM SAUCE

FRESH SALMON STEAKS ARE AS EASY TO COOK AS THEY ARE DELICIOUS.

Melt the 2 tablespoons of butter in the open cooker and gently sauté the shallots for 3 minutes. Add the mushrooms and continue to sauté for 2 minutes then pour in the wine.

Brush the trivet with the melted butter and place the salmon steaks on a sheet of waxed paper and place on the trivet. Place rim-side down into the cooker.

Tie the asparagus into small bundles and place waxed paper on top of the salmon. Place the asparagus bundles on top. Close the lid and bring to 15 lb pressure. Cook for 3 minutes.

Depressurize quickly then remove the asparagus and salmon and keep warm. Blend the cornstarch with the cream and stir into the liquid remaining in the cooker.

Cook, stirring until the sauce thickens. Add seasoning to taste then pour over the salmon. Serve scattered with the scallions and dill.

Serves **4**
Cook control **15 lb**
Preparation time **10 minutes**
Open cooking time **5 minutes**
Pressure cooking time **3 minutes**

2 Tbsp sweet butter plus 1 tsp
  melted butter
4 shallots, peeled and sliced into
  thin wedges
1¼ cups button mushrooms, wiped
  and sliced
1¼ cups oyster mushrooms, wiped
  and chopped if large

1¼ cups dry white wine
Four 5-oz salmon steaks, wiped
8 oz baby asparagus tips, rinsed
1 tsp cornstarch
3 Tbsp light cream
Salt and freshly ground black
  pepper

TO GARNISH
4 scallions, trimmed and
  diagonally sliced
2 Tbsp chopped fresh dill

SPINACH AND PINE NUT-
STUFFED SOLE

FLOUNDER CAN REPLACE THE SOLE IN THIS RECIPE IF PREFERRED.

Heat the oil in the open cooker and sauté the shallots for 3 minutes. Place in a bowl and wipe the cooker clean. Add the remaining stuffing ingredients to the shallots with seasoning to taste and mix to a stiff consistency with the beaten egg.

Lightly rinse or wipe the fish fillets with paper towels and set aside. Discard any tough stalks from the spinach, rinse well, then place in a bowl and pour over boiling water to cover. Leave for 1 to 2 minutes until pliable then drain well.

Place the fillets skin side down on a chopping board and place 2 to 3 spinach leaves on top. Divide the stuffing between the 4 fish fillets, gently spread over each fillet, then roll up starting from the tail end. Secure with toothpicks.

Lightly oil the trivet and place rim-side down in the cooker. Place the fish on top. Mix the wine with the lemon juice and ⅔ cup water and pour over the fish. Close the lid and bring to 15 lb pressure. Cook for 3 minutes then depressurize quickly.

Lift the fish out of the cooker and keep warm. Strain the liquid and return it to the cooker. Blend the butter or margarine and flour to form a paste. Bring the liquid remaining in the cooker to a boil then whisk in small spoonfuls of the paste. Cook, stirring, until a smooth glossy sauce is formed. Roughly chop the shrimp and add to the sauce with the cream. Season to taste. Pour over the fish, garnish, and serve.

Serves **4**
Cook control **15 lb**
Preparation time **20 minutes**
Open cooking time **6 minutes**
Pressure cooking time **3 minutes**

FOR THE STUFFING
1 Tbsp oil
3 shallots, peeled and chopped fine
6 scallions, trimmed and chopped
1 Tbsp grated lemon zest
2 Tbsp toasted pine nuts
¾ cup button mushrooms, chopped
1 cup fresh white bread crumbs
Salt and freshly ground
 black pepper
1 medium egg, beaten

FOR THE FISH
4 large sole fillets, skinned
8 to 12 large spinach leaves
⅔ cup medium-dry white wine
2 Tbsp lemon juice
2 tsp softened butter
 or margarine
2 tsp white all-purpose flour
½ cup peeled shrimp, defrosted
 if frozen
3 Tbsp light cream

TO GARNISH
Fresh herbs and lemon wedges

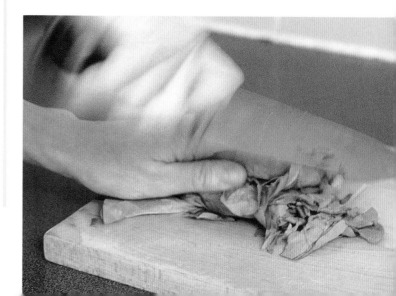

SPICY FISH STEAKS

USE A FIRM FISH FOR THIS RECIPE. FISH SUCH AS FLOUNDER OR SOLE WOULD BE TOO DELICATE AND THEIR FLAVOR WOULD BE COMPLETELY OVERPOWERED. MARINATE THE FISH IN THE REFRIGERATOR FOR SEVERAL HOURS TO INTENSIFY THE SPICY FLAVOR.

Wipe the fish steaks with paper towels and set aside. Mix the spices with seasoning to taste and about 1 tablespoon of oil to form a thick paste then brush over the fish steaks. Place on a plate, cover loosely, and leave in the refrigerator for at least 1 hour, overnight if time permits.

Heat the remaining oil in the open cooker and sauté the onion, garlic, and eggplant for 2 minutes. Add the zucchini and red bell pepper and sauté for a further 2 minutes. Add the tomatoes, seasoning, and 1 tablespoon of the chopped cilantro and pour over the tomato juice.

Place the fish steaks on top and close the lid. Bring to 15 lb pressure and cook for 3 minutes. Depressurize quickly then lift out the fish steaks and vegetables using a slotted spoon and place in a serving dish. Keep warm.

Blend the cornstarch with 1 tablespoon water and stir into the juices left in the cooker. Cook, stirring until the sauce thickens, adjust the seasoning, and pour over the fish. Garnish with the remaining cilantro and serve with fresh cooked rice.

Serves **4**
Cook control **15 lb**
Preparation time **10 minutes**
Open cooking time **5 minutes**
Pressure cooking time **3 minutes**

Four 5-oz fish steaks, such as swordfish, cod, or haddock
1 tsp ground coriander
1 tsp ground cumin
½ to 1 tsp chili powder
Salt and freshly ground black pepper
2 Tbsp oil
1 onion, peeled and chopped
3 to 4 garlic cloves, peeled and crushed

1 small eggplant, about 8 oz in weight, trimmed and diced
2 medium zucchini, trimmed and cut into large dice
1 red bell pepper, seeded and cut into half-moon slices
4 ripe but firm tomatoes, seeded if preferred and cut into quarters
2 Tbsp chopped fresh cilantro
1 cup tomato juice
2 tsp cornstarch

TO SERVE
Rice

COCONUT-FLAVORED HADDOCK

THE COCONUT IN THIS DISH ADDS A BEAUTIFULY CREAMY FLAVOR. IF YOU CANNOT FIND COCONUT MILK EASILY IN YOUR LOCAL STORES, SOAK SOME UNSWEETENED DRIED COCONUT IN ALMOST-BOILING WATER FOR 20 MINUTES, STRAIN, THEN USE THE FLAVORED WATER.

Wipe the fish fillets and place on a sheet of waxed paper. Brush the trivet with the melted butter and place rim-side down into the cooker. Place the fish on the paper onto the trivet and sprinkle with the saffron and the coconut milk. Roughly chop 3 of the scallions and scatter on top of the fish.

Line the separator with foil and add the rice, 2 cups boiling water, corn, and apricots. Finely chop the remaining scallions and chile and add to the rice. Place on top of the fish.

Close the lid and bring to 10 lb pressure. Cook for 5 minutes. Depressurize slowly and lift out the rice and the fish.

Flake the fish into bite-size pieces and stir into the rice with salt and paprika to taste. Add the cilantro, stir lightly, then serve.

Serves **4**
Cook control **10 lb**
Preparation time **15 minutes**
Pressure cooking time
 5 minutes

4 pieces haddock fillet
1 tsp melted butter
A few saffron strands
1¼ cups coconut milk

8 scallions, trimmed
1¼ cups basmati rice
¾ cup corn kernels
¾ cup dried apricots, chopped
1 red chile, seeded and chopped
Salt
Paprika
2 Tbsp chopped fresh cilantro

PROVENÇAL COD LOIN

COD LOIN IS MORE EXPENSIVE THAN FILLET OR CUTLETS,
BUT WELL WORTH THE PRICE BECAUSE YOU GET FIRM, THICK PIECES
OF FISH WITH VERY FEW IF ANY BONES.

Serves **4**
Cook control **15 lb**
Preparation time **5 minutes**
Open cooking time **5 minutes**
Pressure cooking time **3 minutes**

1 Tbsp oil
1 onion, peeled and sliced
4 garlic cloves, peeled and sliced
3 celery stalks, trimmed and sliced
1 green bell pepper, seeded and sliced
1 red bell pepper, seeded and sliced
2 zucchini, trimmed and sliced

One 14-oz can chopped tomatoes
1 Tbsp tomato paste
1 Tbsp chopped fresh oregano
Four 5-oz pieces cod loin
1 tsp cornstarch
Salt and freshly ground black pepper

TO GARNISH
½ cup pitted black olives, chopped
1 Tbsp chopped fresh oregano

TO SERVE
Potatoes or rice, and vegetables

Heat the oil in the open cooker and sauté the onion, garlic, celery, and bell peppers for 3 minutes or until just beginning to soften. Add the zucchini and chopped tomatoes with their juice. Blend the tomato paste with ⅔ cup water and add to the cooker with the oregano. Place the cod on top.

Close the lid and bring to 15 lb pressure. Cook for 3 minutes. Depressurize quickly then lift out the fish and keep warm.

Blend the cornstarch with 1 tablespoon of water and stir into the sauce. Bring to a boil and cook, stirring until thickened then add seasoning to taste.

Pour the sauce over the fish and sprinkle with the chopped olives and oregano. Serve with freshly cooked potatoes or rice, and vegetables.

PROVENÇAL COD LOIN

TROUT WITH HERB BUTTER

IF YOU CANNOT FIND SMALL WHOLE TROUT THAT WILL FIT IN YOUR
PRESSURE COOKER, USE TROUT FILLETS INSTEAD AND COOK
FOR JUST 2 MINUTES.

Serves **4**
Cook control **15 lb**
Preparation time **8 minutes**
Pressure cooking time **3 minutes**

FOR THE BUTTER

1 lemon
¾ stick butter, softened
1 Tbsp chopped fresh parsley
1 Tbsp chopped fresh dill
1 Tbsp snipped fresh chives

FOR THE FISH

4 small 8-oz trout, cleaned
Salt and freshly ground black pepper
1 medium onion, peeled and sliced
4 bay leaves
3 celery stalks, trimmed and chopped
1¼ cups equal parts white wine and
**   water mixed together**

TO GARNISH

Lemon wedges and fresh herb sprigs

TO SERVE

New potatoes and vegetables, and/or
**   salad**

Grate the zest from the lemon, reserve the zest, and thin slice the lemon. Cream
the softened butter with the lemon zest and chopped herbs, shape into a roll,
wrap in waxed paper, and chill in the refrigerator until required.

Rinse the trout and pat dry with paper towels. Season the cavities with salt and
pepper and place a little of the sliced onion in each fish cavity with a bay leaf.
Then place half a slice of lemon in each cavity and press the flesh together.

Place the remaining onion, sliced lemon, and chopped celery in the open cooker
and place the trout on top. Pour over the wine and water and close the lid.

Bring to 15 lb pressure and cook for 3 minutes. Depressurize quickly then remove
the trout from the cooker. Place a quarter of the herb butter on top of each fish
and garnish with lemon wedges and herb sprigs. Serve with new potatoes and
fresh cooked vegetables, and/or salad.

WARM TUNA AND PASTA SALAD

IF FRESH TUNA IS UNAVAILABLE, USE SWORDFISH OR SALMON STEAKS INSTEAD. TAKE CARE NOT TO OVERCOOK FRESH TUNA OR IT WILL BECOME DRY AND TASTELESS.

Heat the oil in the open cooker and sauté the onion, chile, and celery for 3 minutes, add the chopped bell peppers with the eggplant and continue to sauté for 4 minutes. Add the chopped tomatoes with their juice and the black olives.

Lightly oil the trivet then place it rim-side down into the cooker. Place the tuna steaks on top.

Line the separator with foil, add the pasta and 2 cups water, and place on top of the tuna. Close the lid, bring to 15 lb pressure and cook for 5 minutes. Depressurize quickly and lift out the pasta and tuna. Drain the pasta, place into a bowl, and stir. Flake the tuna into bite-size pieces and add to the pasta together with the cooked vegetables. Season to taste. Stir lightly then serve warm, sprinkled with the shredded basil and shavings of Parmesan cheese, if using.

Serves **6**
Cook control **15 lb**
Preparation time **10 minutes**
Open cooking time **7 minutes**
Pressure cooking time **5 minutes**

1 Tbsp olive oil
1 onion, peeled and cut into wedges
1 small jalapeño chile, seeded
  and chopped
3 celery stalks, trimmed and sliced
1 red bell pepper, seeded and chopped
1 green bell pepper, seeded and chopped
1 small eggplant, trimmed and chopped
One 14-oz can chopped tomatoes
1 cup pitted black olives
1 lb fresh tuna steak
Generous 1½ cups dried pasta shapes
  such as farfalle or twists
Salt and freshly ground black pepper

TO GARNISH
2 Tbsp shredded basil

TO SERVE
Shavings of Parmesan cheese (optional)

SMOKED HADDOCK PILAF

I ALWAYS USE UNDYED SMOKED HADDOCK BECAUSE IN MY OPINION, THE FLAVOR IS FAR SUPERIOR, BUT IT IS A QUESTION OF PERSONAL TASTE, SO USE WHICHEVER YOU PREFER. THIS RECIPE WILL WORK WELL WITH EITHER.

Pour 1¼ cups of water into the pressure cooker and place the trivet in rim-side down. Line the separator with foil, add the peas and rice, and pour over 2 cups of the broth. Close the lid and bring to 15 lb pressure and cook for 5 minutes. Depressurize slowly then remove the peas and rice and keep warm. Remove the trivet and wipe the cooker clean.

Heat the oil in the open cooker and sauté the bacon, onion, garlic, and celery for 3 minutes. Stir in the red bell pepper and mushrooms, chopped tomatoes, and the remaining broth and place the fish on top.

Close the lid and bring to 15 lb pressure and cook for 5 minutes. Depressurize quickly then lift out the separator and transfer to a warm serving dish. Flake the fish into bite-size pieces and mix into the cooked rice with the vegetables. Add seasoning to taste. Serve immediately, garnished with the parsley sprigs.

Serves **4**
Cook control **15 lb**
Preparation time **15 minutes**
Open cooking time **3 minutes**
Pressure cooking time **10 minutes**

½ cup frozen peas
1 cup long-grain rice
2½ cups fish or vegetable broth
1 Tbsp oil
8 slices bacon, chopped
1 medium onion, peeled and chopped
3 garlic cloves, peeled and chopped
3 celery stalks, trimmed and chopped
1 red bell pepper, seeded and chopped
4 large field mushrooms, trimmed and chopped
One 14-oz can chopped tomatoes
12 oz smoked haddock fillet, skinned
Salt and freshly ground black pepper

TO GARNISH
Flat-leaf parsley sprigs

ORIENTAL SEA BASS

IF YOU CAN FIND SMALL WHOLE SEA BASS THAT WILL FIT INTO THE PRESSURE COOKER, USE THEM. OTHERWISE, USE FILLETS TO ENSURE THAT THE FISH IS DONE AND LOOKS ATTRACTIVE WHEN SERVED.

Rinse the fish, pat dry, and reserve. Mix together the grated gingerroot, garlic, lemon grass, and chile. Place in the fish cavity or on the fillets and roll up loosely then top with the star anise and the shredded scallions.

Lightly oil the trivet, set it in the cooker rim-side down, and place the fish on top. Mix the broth with the sake or sherry and pour over the fish.

Line the separator with foil and add the rice then pour in 2 cups boiling water. Place in the cooker on top of the fish. Close the lid and bring quickly to 15 lb pressure. Cook for 5 minutes.

Depressurize quickly then remove the rice and fish and keep warm. Strain the cooking liquid and return to the cleaned cooker, and bring to a boil. Blend the cornstarch with 1 tablespoon of water then stir into the boiling liquid. Cook, stirring until thickened.

Arrange the rice on warm individual serving plates, top with the fish, pour over a little of the sauce and serve the remainder separately. Garnish with cilantro sprigs, and serve immediately, with the salad.

Serves **4**
Cook control **15 lb**
Preparation time **10 minutes**
Pressure cooking time **5 minutes**

4 small whole sea bass or four 8-oz sea bass or similar fish fillets, cleaned and descaled if necessary
One 2-in piece fresh gingerroot, peeled and grated
2 large garlic cloves, peeled and crushed
3 lemon grass stalks, outer leaves discarded and chopped very fine
1 serrano chile, seeded and fine chopped

8 star anise
6 large scallions, trimmed and shredded
1 tsp oil
1 cup fish or vegetable broth
¼ cup sake or dry sherry
1¼ cups fragrant Thai rice
1 tsp cornstarch

TO GARNISH
Cilantro sprigs

TO SERVE
Chinese-style green leaf salad

NAVARIN OF ANGLER FISH
WITH SPRING VEGETABLES

ANGLER FISH MAY LOOK VERY UGLY BUT ITS FIRM FLESH MAKES IT A SUPERB FISH
TO COOK WITH AND ONE THAT WORKS WELL WITH ROBUST FLAVORS.

Discard the central bone and any skin from the angler fish, rinse lightly, then cut into small pieces. Season well and set aside. Cut all the root vegetables into even-size pieces and set aside.

Heat the oil in the open cooker and gently sauté the vegetables except the fava beans and zucchini for 3 minutes. Add the beans and zucchini and sauté for 1 minute then add the bouquet garni to the cooker.

Blend the tomato paste with the broth then pour over the vegetables and add a little seasoning. Place the fish pieces on top and sprinkle with 1 tablespoon of the dill. Close the lid and bring to 15 lb pressure. Cook for 3 minutes.

Depressurize quickly then adjust the seasoning and remove the cooked vegetables and fish and keep warm.

Blend the butter and flour together to form a paste then whisk small spoonfuls into the liquid remaining in the cooker. Bring to a boil, whisking, and cook until thickened. Pour over the fish and vegetables then serve sprinkled with the remaining chopped dill.

Serves **4**
Cook control **15 lb**
Preparation time **20 minutes**
Open cooking time **4 minutes**
Pressure cooking time **3 minutes**

One 1½-lb piece angler fish tail
Salt and freshly ground black pepper
8 baby onions, peeled
4 baby turnips, peeled
10 oz baby potatoes, scrubbed
10 oz baby carrots, scrubbed
1 Tbsp oil
1 cup shelled fava beans
6 oz baby zucchini, trimmed
1 bouquet garni
2 Tbsp tomato paste
1¼ cups vegetable broth
2 Tbsp chopped fresh dill
1 Tbsp softened butter
1 Tbsp white all-purpose flour

MEAT

SWEET-AND-SOUR PORK
WITH PINEAPPLE

WHETHER YOU ARE COOKING FOR THE FAMILY OR ENTERTAINING FRIENDS, THIS COLORFUL PORK DISH IS AN IDEAL CHOICE. BY USING YOUR PRESSURE COOKER, YOU CAN HAVE IT READY IN MINUTES.

Heat the oil in the open cooker then sauté the pork for 5 minutes or until sealed. Remove with a slotted spoon and reserve. Add the onions and garlic and sauté for 5 minutes or until softened. Remove and drain off any excess oil.

Return the pork and onions to the cooker with the carrots, bell pepper strips, and mushrooms.

Drain the juice from the pineapple and set aside the pineapple. Make the juice up to 1¼ cups with water. Blend the ketchup, soy sauce, vinegar, and sugar together then stir in the pineapple juice and pour in the cooker.

Close the lid, bring to 15 lb pressure quickly and cook for 5 minutes. Depressurize quickly then stir in the reserved pineapple.

Blend the cornstarch with 1 tablespoon water and stir into the cooker. Bring to a boil, stirring until thickened. Add seasoning to taste, sprinkle with the cashews and parsley, and serve with the rice or potatoes.

Serves **4**
Cook control **15 lb**
Preparation time **15 minutes**
Open cooking time **15 minutes**
Pressure cooking time **5 minutes**

1 Tbsp oil
1 lb pork fillet, trimmed and cubed
2 red onions, peeled and cut into wedges
4 garlic cloves, peeled and sliced
8 oz carrots, peeled and cut into thin strips
1 red bell pepper, seeded and cut into strips
1 yellow bell pepper, seeded and cut into strips
1½ cups wild or button mushrooms, wiped and sliced if large
One 7-oz can pineapple pieces
2 Tbsp ketchup
1 Tbsp light soy sauce
1 Tbsp white wine vinegar
2 tsp granulated brown sugar
1 Tbsp cornstarch
Salt and freshly ground black pepper
½ cup cashews, toasted

TO GARNISH
1 Tbsp chopped fresh flat-leaf parsley

TO SERVE
Rice or new potatoes

BARBECUED PORK RIBS

PROVIDE PLENTY OF PAPER NAPKINS AND SOME FINGER BOWLS FOR YOUR GUESTS
WHEN SERVING THESE DELICIOUS RIBS.

Serves **4**
Cook control **15 lb**
Preparation time **5 minutes**
Open cooking time **10 minutes**
Pressure cooking time **10 minutes**

2 Tbsp oil
2 lb Chinese-style pork ribs
1 large onion, peeled and chopped
4 to 6 garlic cloves, peeled and crushed
4 celery stalks, trimmed and sliced
2 Tbsp tomato paste
1 Tbsp Dijon mustard
1 Tbsp dark corn syrup
4 Tbsp granulated brown sugar
1 cup chicken or vegetable broth
1 cup cherry tomatoes

TO SERVE
Shredded bok choy or similar
  Oriental leaf

Heat 1 tablespoon of the oil in the open cooker and brown the ribs on all sides. Remove from the cooker and set aside. Clean the pan then add the remaining oil and add the onion, garlic, and celery to the cooker. Sauté for 5 minutes then return the ribs to the cooker.

Blend the tomato paste, mustard, dark corn syrup, sugar, and broth and pour over the ribs. Add the cherry tomatoes and close the lid.

Bring the cooker to 15 lb pressure and cook for 10 minutes. Depressurize quickly and either serve immediately on a bed of shredded Oriental leaves or arrange on a foil-lined broiler pan and cook under a preheated broiler for 10 minutes, turning over at least once, until the ribs are crisp.

PORK AND APRICOT CASSEROLE

DRIED APRICOTS ARE ONE OF MY ALL-TIME FAVORITE INGREDIENTS AND THEY FEATURE IN MANY OF MY DISHES. HERE I HAVE COMBINED THEM WITH CIDER TO GIVE THE PORK AN UNUSUAL, INTERESTING FLAVOR.

Serves **4**
Cook control **15 lb**
Preparation time **10 minutes**
Open cooking time **6 minutes**
Pressure cooking time
  15 minutes

1 lb pork fillet
1 Tbsp oil
1 medium onion, peeled and sliced
3 to 4 garlic cloves, peeled and sliced
¼ cup dried apricots, chopped
2 medium carrots, peeled and cut into batons
1 yellow bell pepper, seeded and cut into half-moon shapes
1 bouquet garni
2 cups sweet cider
1 Tbsp dark soy sauce
Salt and freshly ground black pepper
2 tsp cornstarch

TO GARNISH
Fresh apricots if available and fresh sage leaves

TO SERVE
Freshly cooked vegetables

Trim off any fat from the pork and cut into small pieces. Heat the oil in the open cooker and sauté the onion, garlic, apricots, and carrots for 2 minutes. Remove from the cooker with a slotted spoon and reserve. Add the pork to the cooker and cook, stirring for 2 minutes or until sealed.

Return the onion mixture to the cooker and add the yellow bell pepper and bouquet garni then pour in the cider. Stir well.

Close the lid and bring to 15 lb pressure. Cook for 15 minutes. Depressurize quickly then add soy sauce with seasoning to taste. Blend the cornstarch with 1 tablespoon of extra cider or water and stir into the open cooker. Place over a gentle heat and cook, stirring until slightly thickened. Remove the bouquet garni and garnish with apricots and sage. Serve with freshly cooked vegetables.

PORK WITH PRUNE
AND ORANGE STUFFING

YOU HAVE TO ADOPT A SLIGHTLY DIFFERENT ATTITUDE TO SEASONING WHEN COOKING WITH A PRESSURE COOKER. I HAVE FOUND THAT UNLESS YOU USE PLENTY OF SEASONING THE FOOD CAN BE QUITE BLAND, SO ADD SEASONING BEFORE COOKING, BUT ALWAYS CHECK AND ADJUST AFTERWARD, BEFORE SERVING.

Cut along the length of the pork chops along the fat edge to form a pocket.

Heat the oil in the open cooker and brown the chops on all sides (you may need to do this in 2 batches). Remove from the cooker and cool while preparing the stuffing.

Mix together the chopped prunes, orange zest, pecans, rice, and sage with seasoning, stir in the egg yolk then stuff the pork chops with the mixture.

Place the pork chops in the cooker and add the orange juice and white wine.

Close the lid and bring to 15 lb pressure. Cook for 15 minutes. Depressurize quickly then remove from the cooker and keep warm.

Add the marmalade to the liquid remaining in the cooker, bring to a boil, and boil for 2 to 3 minutes or until the sauce becomes syrupy. Pour the sauce over the chops and garnish with the fresh sage leaves and sliced plums. Serve with freshly cooked vegetables or salad.

Serves **4**
Cook control **15 lb**
Preparation time **10 minutes**
Open cooking time **8 minutes**
Pressure cooking time
  15 minutes

4 boneless pork chops
1 Tbsp oil
½ cup dried prunes, chopped
1 Tbsp grated orange zest
2 Tbsp pecans, chopped
¼ cup cooked long-grain rice
1 Tbsp chopped fresh sage

Salt and freshly ground black
  pepper
1 small egg yolk
⅔ cup orange juice
⅔ cup dry white wine
2 Tbsp fine-cut orange
  marmalade

TO GARNISH
Fresh sage leaves and sliced
  fresh plums

TO SERVE
Vegetables or salad

PAPRIKA PORK

COMFORT FOOD IS ALWAYS APPRECIATED WHEN THE WEATHER TURNS COLDER
AND THIS PORK DISH IS CERTAINLY WARM, FILLING, AND SUSTAINING.

Heat the oil in the open cooker and sauté the onion and garlic for 2 minutes. Add the pork and continue to sauté until the pork is completely sealed. Add the red and green bell peppers and sprinkle in the paprika. Sauté for 2 minutes before adding the contents of the can of tomatoes, a little salt, and ⅔ cup of the broth. Close the lid and bring to 15 lb pressure. Cook for 8 minutes then depressurize quickly and remove the lid. Stir in the eggplant.

Place the trivet rim-side down on top of the pork and line the separator with foil. Place the noodles into the separator and pour over the remaining broth. Place on the trivet. Close the lid and return to 15 lb pressure. Cook for 5 minutes then depressurize quickly.

Remove the separator and drain the pasta noodles if necessary and place on a warmed serving platter.

Adjust the seasoning of the pork and stir the sour cream and chopped parsley into the cooked meat. Spoon on top of the cooked pasta and serve.

Serves **6**
Cook control **15 lb**
Preparation time **10 minutes**
Open cooking time **7 minutes**
Pressure cooking time **13 minutes**

2 Tbsp oil
1 large onion, peeled and sliced
3 to 4 garlic cloves, peeled and crushed
1½ lb pork cubes
1 red bell pepper, seeded and cut into half moons
1 green bell pepper, seeded and cut into half moons
1 Tbsp paprika
One 14-oz can chopped tomatoes
Salt
2½ cups pork or vegetable broth
1 small eggplant, about 8 oz in weight, trimmed and diced
8 oz pasta noodles
⅔ cup sour cream
2 Tbsp chopped fresh parsley

BOSTON BAKED BEANS WITH PORK

THE BENEFITS OF USING A PRESSURE COOKER CAN BE SEEN CLEARLY IN THIS DISH, WHICH WOULD NORMALLY TAKE 3 TO 4 HOURS TO COOK. THE COOKING TIME IS DRASTICALLY REDUCED, WITHOUT AFFECTING THE FLAVOR.

Serves **4**
Cook control **15 lb**
Preparation time **10 minutes plus 1 hour soaking**
Open cooking time **5 minutes**
Pressure cooking time **18 minutes**

1 cup dried navy beans
1 Tbsp oil
2 medium onions, peeled and chopped
4 garlic cloves, peeled and chopped
1 lb pork belly, diced
1 tsp mustard powder
½ tsp ground cinnamon
¼ tsp ground cloves
1 Tbsp dark corn syrup
1 Tbsp red wine vinegar
2 Tbsp tomato paste
One 14-oz can chopped tomatoes
1 cup vegetable or chicken broth
Salt and freshly ground black pepper

TO GARNISH
2 Tbsp chopped fresh parsley

Cover the beans with boiling water and soak for 1 hour. Drain and set aside.

Heat the oil in the open cooker and sauté the onions, garlic, and diced pork for 5 minutes. Blend the mustard and spices with the dark corn syrup, vinegar, and tomato paste and pour into the cooker. Add the beans with the chopped tomatoes and their juice, the broth, and seasoning.

Close the lid and bring to 15 lb pressure. Cook for 18 minutes.

Depressurize slowly then stir in the chopped parsley and serve.

LAMB WITH PINTO BEANS

THIS RECIPE PROVIDES A WONDERFUL WARMING MEAL THAT IS JUST RIGHT FOR WHEN THE DAYS ARE BECOMING A LITTLE CHILLY. FOR EXTRA HEAT SIMPLY ADD A CHOPPED CHILE OR TWO TO THE ONION, GARLIC, AND FENNEL AT THE BEGINNING OF THE RECIPE.

Serves **4**
Cook control **15 lb**
Preparation time **8 minutes plus 1 hour soaking time**
Open cooking time **6 minutes**
Pressure cooking time **12 minutes**

1 cup dried pinto beans
1 Tbsp oil
4 double loin lamb chops
1 medium onion, peeled and cut into wedges
4 garlic cloves, peeled and sliced
1 head fennel, trimmed and sliced
One 14-oz can chopped tomatoes
2 to 3 tsp Worcestershire sauce
1 Tbsp paprika
1 Tbsp tomato paste
1¼ cups beef broth
Salt
2 Tbsp chopped fresh parsley

TO SERVE
Crusty bread and green salad

Cover the beans with boiling water and soak for 1 hour. Drain and set aside.

Heat the oil in the open cooker and brown the lamb chops on all sides. Remove from the cooker and set aside.

Add the onion, garlic, and fennel to the cooker and sauté for 3 minutes then stir in the drained beans, the contents of the can of chopped tomatoes, the Worcestershire sauce, and paprika.

Blend the tomato paste with the broth and stir into the bean mixture, place the lamb chops on top, and bring to a boil. Close the lid, bring to 15 lb pressure and cook for 12 minutes.

Depressurize slowly then remove the lamb chops. Add salt to taste to the bean mixture then stir in the chopped parsley and serve the lamb chops with the beans, crusty bread, and a green salad.

SPICED BEEF POT ROAST

THIS JOINT IS EQUALLY DELICIOUS WHETHER IT IS SERVED HOT OR COLD. WHEN COLD, IT MAKES AN IDEAL DISH TO SERVE FOR BUFFETS, PICNICS, OR WITH SALAD WHEN DINING AL FRESCO.

Heat the oil in the open cooker and brown the joint on all sides. Remove from the cooker. Add the vegetables to the cooker and sauté for 5 minutes then remove with a slotted spoon and drain off any excess oil from the pan.

Add the broth and the wine and water mixture, stirring well to loosen any residue sticking to the pan then place the trivet rim-side down in the cooker and place the joint onto the trivet. Arrange the vegetables around the meat.

Sprinkle the spices into the pan with the sugar and close the lid. Bring to 15 lb pressure and cook for 45 minutes.

Depressurize quickly then lift out the joint and vegetables and place on warmed serving plate and keep warm. Sprinkle the vegetables with the parsley just before serving.

Meanwhile strain the liquid in the pan then bring to a boil. Blend the cornstarch with 1 tablespoon water and stir into the boiling liquor. Cook, stirring for 2 to 3 minutes or until thickened. Serve with the joint and vegetables.

Serves **6**
Cook control **15 lb**
Preparation time **15 minutes**
Open cooking time **10 minutes**
Pressure cooking time **45 minutes**

1 Tbsp oil
One 3-lb brisket or similar pot roasting joint
2 turnips, peeled and cut into chunks
2 large carrots, peeled and cut into chunks
10 baby onions, peeled
3 celery stalks, trimmed and sliced into chunks
1¼ cups beef broth
1¼ cups red wine and water mixed
About 10 cloves
2 bay leaves
1 cinnamon stick, bruised
1 small piece gingerroot, chopped
1 Tbsp granulated brown sugar
1 Tbsp chopped fresh parsley
1 Tbsp cornstarch

LIVER WITH MARSALA

MARSALA WINE IS A FORTIFIED WINE USED IN THE ITALIAN DESSERT, ZABAGLIONE. HERE I HAVE USED IT WITH LIVER GIVING A DELICIOUS RICH AND LUSCIOUS SAUCE NEEDING PLENTY OF BREAD OR POTATOES TO MOP UP.

Cut the liver into thin strips, rinse, and pat dry with paper towels. Heat 1 tablespoon of the oil in the open cooker and brown the liver on all sides. Remove from the cooker and rinse the cooker. Add the remaining oil then the onion and garlic to the cooker and sauté for 3 minutes. Add the broth, wine, and red currant jelly then arrange the liver on top.

Place the trivet rim-side down into the cooker and place the potatoes on top. Close the lid and bring to 15 lb pressure. Cook for 3 minutes. Depressurize quickly and remove the lid.

Put the broccoli into the separator, place on top of the potatoes, close the lid, and return to 15 lb pressure. Cook for 2 minutes then depressurize quickly.

Remove the vegetables and liver from the cooker, place in warm serving dishes, and keep warm.

Blend the butter and flour together to form a paste and bring the liquid remaining in the cooker to a boil. Whisk small spoonfuls of the flour paste into the liquid and continue whisking until the sauce has thickened and is smooth. Add seasoning to taste then pour over the liver, garnish, and serve with the cooked vegetables.

Serves **4**
Cook control **15 lb**
Preparation time **10 minutes**
Open cooking time **5 minutes**
Pressure cooking time **5 minutes**

1¼ lb lamb liver, trimmed

2 Tbsp oil

1 medium onion, peeled and sliced

2 garlic cloves, peeled and sliced

1 cup lamb or vegetable broth

¼ cup Marsala wine

1 Tbsp red currant jelly

1½ lb potatoes, peeled and cut into chunks

12 oz broccoli florets

1 Tbsp softened butter

1 Tbsp white all-purpose flour

Salt and freshly ground black pepper

TO GARNISH
Flat-leaf parsley sprigs

BEEF IN SOUR CREAM SAUCE

THERE ARE MANY TYPES OF CHILE AVAILABLE, I HAVE SUGGESTED JALAPEÑOS FOR THIS RECIPE BECAUSE THEY ARE EXTREMELY EASY TO FIND, BUT YOU CAN SUBSTITUTE SERRANOS OR ANOTHER VARIETY IF YOU PREFER.

Trim the steak, cut it into thin strips, and set aside. Heat 1 tablespoon of the oil in the open cooker then sauté the onions, garlic, and chile for 3 minutes. Add the mushrooms and bell pepper strips and continue to sauté for a further 2 minutes. Remove the vegetables from the cooker using a slotted spoon and reserve.

Add the remaining oil to the cooker then add the beef strips to the open cooker and cook for 3 to 5 minutes or until sealed, then return the onions and mushrooms to the cooker.

Blend the mustard, tomato paste, and broth together then pour into the cooker. Add a little seasoning and nutmeg then close the lid.

Bring to 15 lb pressure and cook for 8 minutes. Depressurize quickly then adjust the seasoning. Stir in the sour cream and parsley, stir well, and serve.

Serves **4**
Cook control **15 lb**
Preparation time **10 minutes**
Open cooking time **8 minutes**
Pressure cooking time **8 minutes**

1 lb beef top round steak
2 Tbsp oil
2 red onions, peeled and cut into wedges
3 to 4 garlic cloves, peeled and crushed
1 small red jalapeño chile, seeded and chopped

1½ cups assorted wild mushrooms, wiped and sliced if large
1 red bell pepper, seeded and sliced
1 tsp dry mustard
1 Tbsp tomato paste
1 cup beef broth
Salt and freshly ground black pepper
¼ tsp grated fresh nutmeg
4 Tbsp sour cream
1 Tbsp chopped fresh flat-leaf parsley

BEEF WITH CAPER DUMPLINGS

WHEN PLACING MEAT, FISH, OR ANY OTHER FOODS ONTO THE TRIVET, IT IS A GOOD IDEA
TO LIGHLY OIL THE TRIVET FIRST. YOU CAN ALSO PLACE THE FOOD ON A PIECE OF WAXED PAPER,
WHICH MAKES IT EASY TO REMOVE ONCE COOKED.

Heat the oil in the open cooker and brown the joint on all sides. Remove from the cooker and wipe the cooker clean. Place the trivet rim-side down in the cooker and place the joint on top then add the bay leaves and mixed herbs.

Pour in the broth, close the lid, and bring to 15 lb pressure. Cook for 30 minutes.

Meanwhile prepare the vegetables and set aside. Mix the self-rising flour and suet together and stir in the capers, parsley, and seasoning to taste. Mix to a soft dough with 6 to 7 tablespoons cold water. Form into 8 small balls and reserve.

Depressurize the meat quickly, remove the lid and arrange the prepared vegetables around the joint, and close the lid.

Return to 15 lb pressure and cook for 5 minutes. Depressurize quickly and remove the vegetables and meat. Place on warmed serving dishes and keep warm. Place the dumplings on the trivet and return the cooker to the heat. Close the lid, but do not bring to pressure, and cook for 10 minutes or until the dumplings are fluffy and done. Remove from the cooker and place with the meat and vegetables.

Blend the cornstarch with 2 tablespoons of water then stir into the liquid remaining in the open cooker. Cook, stirring until the liquid thickens then serve with the meat, vegetables, and dumplings.

Serves **6**
Cook control **15 lb**
Preparation time **15 minutes**
Open cooking time **18 minutes**
Pressure cooking time
　35 minutes

1 Tbsp oil
3 lb rolled beef pot roasting joint
2 bay leaves
2 Tbsp chopped fresh mixed herbs
2½ cups hot broth
2 medium carrots, peeled and cut into chunks
6 oz turnips, peeled and cut into chunks
2 leeks, trimmed and sliced
8 oz parsnips, peeled and cut into chunks
10 oz potatoes, peeled and cut into chunks
1½ cups self-rising flour
½ cup suet or solid vegetable shortening
2 Tbsp capers, drained and chopped
1 Tbsp chopped fresh parsley
Salt and freshly ground black pepper
1 Tbsp cornstarch

STUFFED GRAPE LEAVES

WHEN USING GRAPE LEAVES THAT HAVE BEEN PRESERVED IN BRINE,
IT IS IMPORTANT TO SOAK THEM WELL IN ORDER TO REMOVE THE TASTE OF THE BRINE.

Cover the grape leaves in almost-boiling water, leave for 20 minutes, drain well, and pat dry with paper towels.

Heat the oil in the open cooker and sauté the shallots, garlic, and ground lamb for 5 minutes or until the lamb is sealed. Remove from the cooker and drain off any excess oil then place in a bowl. Wipe the base of the cooker clean.

Add the apricots, raisins, one tablespoon of orange zest, seasoning to taste, and the chopped cilantro. Mix well.

Place 2 to 3 grape leaves on a chopping board and place a spoonful of the lamb mixture on top. Roll up, encasing the mixture, and secure with fine twine. Repeat until all the grape leaves and ground lamb mixture have been used.

Blend the tomato paste with the $^2/_3$ cup broth and pour into the cooker. Place the trivet into the cooker rim-side down and place the stuffed grape leaves on top.

Line the separator with foil. Mix the rice with the remaining orange zest and chopped red bell pepper and place into the foil-lined separator. Pour in the remaining broth and cover with foil. Secure firmly. Place on top of the grape leaves.

Close the lid and bring to 15 lb pressure. Cook for 5 minutes. Depressurize quickly then arrange the rice in a warm serving platter, top with the grape leaves, garnish, and serve.

Serves **4**
Cook control **15 lb**
Preparation time **15 minutes**
    plus 20 minutes soaking
Open cooking time **5 minutes**
Pressure cooking time **5 minutes**

One package preserved grape
    leaves (about 20)
1 Tbsp oil
3 shallots, peeled and chopped fine
2 garlic cloves, peeled and crushed
10 oz ground lamb
½ cup dried apricots, chopped
½ cup raisins
2 Tbsp grated orange zest

Salt and freshly ground
    black pepper
1 Tbsp chopped fresh cilantro
1 Tbsp tomato paste
3 cups lamb or vegetable broth
1 cup long-grain rice
1 red bell pepper, seeded
    and chopped

TO GARNISH
Fresh cilantro sprigs

FARMHOUSE PÂTÉ

A CERTAIN AMOUNT OF LIQUID WILL OOZE OUT OF THE PÂTÉ AFTER IT IS DONE BUT
THIS WILL FLOW BACK INTO THE MEAT ON COOLING AND ENSURE THAT IT REMAINS MOIST.

Serves **8**
Cook control **15 lb**
Preparation time **25 minutes plus overnight chilling time**
Pressure cooking time
   25 minutes

8 slices bacon
4 shallots, peeled and chopped
4 garlic cloves, peeled and crushed
4 oz lamb or beef liver, chopped
8 oz ground pork
4 oz sausage meat
2 Tbsp chopped fresh mixed herbs
Salt and freshly ground black pepper
¼ tsp freshly grated nutmeg
2 Tbsp brandy
1 Tbsp lemon juice

TO SERVE
Salad and crusty bread

Line a 3-cup ovenproof pan with some of the bacon slices, reserving the remainder. Mix the shallots, garlic, chopped lamb liver, ground pork, and sausage meat until blended. Add the mixed herbs, seasoning, and nutmeg, then stir in the brandy. Spoon the mixture into the bacon-lined pan and arrange the remaining bacon on top. Cover with a double layer of waxed paper and secure.

Place the trivet rim-side down in the cooker and add 2 cups water with the lemon juice. Stand the dish on the trivet, close the lid, and bring to 15 lb pressure. Cook for 25 minutes, depressurize quickly, then take it out. Cover with waxed paper, cool, then leave overnight in the refrigerator pressed down with a weight. Unmold and serve.

GINGER AND ORANGE PORK

A MOIST AND SUCCULENT PORK JOINT IS PERFECT TO SERVE FOR A DINNER PARTY OR FAMILY GET-TOGETHER.

Serves **6 to 8**
Cook control **15 lb**
Preparation time **10 minutes**
Open cooking time **10 minutes plus 5 minutes standing time**
Pressure cooking time
   24 minutes plus 15 minutes in oven

One 3-lb boneless pork joint
One 3-in piece gingerroot, sliced
1 onion, peeled and cut into quarters
1 carrot, peeled and cut into chunks
About 26 cloves

Pared zest of 1 orange
3 Tbsp raw brown sugar
1 tsp ground ginger
1¼ cups orange juice
2 Tbsp soy sauce
1 Tbsp cornstarch
2 tsp grated orange zest
Freshly ground black pepper

TO GARNISH
Orange wedges and parsley sprigs

TO SERVE
Freshly cooked vegetables

Place the joint in the open cooker and pour in sufficient water to half-fill, then add the sliced gingerroot, onion, carrot, about 6 of the whole cloves, and the orange zest. Close the lid and bring to 15 lb pressure.

Cook for 24 minutes, depressurize quickly and remove the meat. Reserve ⅔ cup of the cooking liquid. Allow to cool a little, strip off the skin, and score the fat into a diamond pattern. Stud the scored fat with cloves.

Preheat the oven to 400°F. Place the meat in a roasting pan. Mix the sugar and ground ginger together and press onto the scored fat. Pour over the orange juice, the reserved cooking liquid, and the soy sauce. Bake for 15 minutes or until the top is crisp, basting the joint occasionally with the juices in the pan. When done, remove the joint from the pan and keep warm.

Pour the juices into a saucepan and bring to a boil. Blend the cornstarch with 1 tablespoon water and stir into the boiling liquid. Stir until slightly thickened. Add the orange zest with seasoning to taste then serve with the meat, garnished with orange and parsley and cooked vegetables.

BEEF OLIVES

IF YOU DO NOT HAVE A MEAT MALLET, A ROLLING PIN WORKS JUST AS WELL. PLACE THE STEAKS
BETWEEN 2 SHEETS OF WAXED PAPER SO THEY DO NOT TEAR WHILE BEING POUNDED.

Place the steaks between 2 sheets of waxed paper and pound
with a meat mallet until about $1/4$ inch thin. Set aside.

Heat 1 tablespoon of the oil in the open cooker and sauté
the shallots and garlic for 3 minutes. Add the mushrooms
and continue to sauté for 2 minutes or until the mushrooms
have wilted. Remove from the heat and stir in the bread
crumbs, orange zest, thyme, and pine nuts with seasoning
to taste. Stir in the beaten egg and mix to a stiff consistency.
Divide between the four pieces of steak and roll up and secure
with fine twine.

Wipe the cooker clean, heat the remaining oil, and brown
the beef rolls on all sides. Remove and drain off any excess
oil then replace the beef rolls and pour in the red wine and
$2/3$ cup of water.

Close the lid and bring to 15 lb pressure. Cook for 15 minutes.
Depressurize quickly and place the beef rolls onto a warmed
serving dish. Keep warm.

Blend the butter and flour together to form a paste. Add the
remaining water to the liquid in the cooker, bring to a boil,
and whisk small spoonfuls of the paste into the boiling liquid.
Cook, still whisking, until a smooth, glossy, and slightly
thickened sauce is formed. Add the red wine jelly or red
currant jelly to the sauce, adjust the seasoning, and serve
with the garnished beef olives and freshly cooked vegetables.

Serves **4**
Cook control **15 lb**
Preparation time **15 minutes**
Open cooking time **10 minutes**
Pressure cooking time
   15 minutes

4 thin slices steak
2 Tbsp oil
3 shallots, peeled and chopped
2 garlic cloves, peeled
   and crushed
1¼ cups mushrooms, wiped and
   chopped
¾ cup fresh white bread crumbs
1 Tbsp grated orange zest
1 Tbsp chopped fresh thyme

3 Tbsp pine nuts
Salt and freshly ground
   black pepper
1 small egg, beaten
1¼ cups red wine
1¼ cups water
1 Tbsp softened butter
1 Tbsp white all-purpose flour
3 to 4 tsp red wine jelly or red
   currant jelly

TO GARNISH
Orange zest

TO SERVE
Freshly cooked vegetables

LAMB WITH EGGPLANT

BULGUR WHEAT, ALSO KNOWN AS CRACKED WHEAT, IS A PROCESSED WHEAT POPULAR THROUGHOUT THE MIDDLE EAST. IT IS MOST COMMONLY USED IN TABBOULEH, A LEBANESE SALAD.

Trim the lamb, dice fine, and set aside. Heat 1 tablespoon of the oil in the open cooker and sauté the lamb for 5 minutes or until sealed. Remove the lamb from the pan using a slotted spoon and set aside.

Add the remaining oil to the cooker then add the onions, garlic, eggplant, and orange bell pepper and sauté for 1 minute.

Return the lamb to the cooker with the chopped tomatoes and their juice, and the broth, and add seasoning to taste. Close the lid and bring to 15 lb pressure and cook for 10 minutes.

Meanwhile line the separator with foil and add the bulgur wheat mixed with the raisins, pine nuts, and lemon zest. Pour in 2 cups of water, cover with waxed paper, and secure.

Quickly depressurize the cooker, place the separator on top of the lamb then close the lid and return to pressure. Cook for 5 minutes.

Slowly depressurize the cooker and remove the bulgur wheat and lamb. Fluff up the bulgur wheat with a fork and spoon onto a warmed serving dish together with the cooked lamb. Sprinkle with the chopped cilantro and serve.

Serves **4**
Cook control **15 lb**
Preparation time **10 minutes**
Open cooking time **6 minutes**
Pressure cooking time **15 minutes**

1 lb lamb fillet
2 Tbsp oil
2 medium onions, peeled and cut into wedges
4 garlic cloves, peeled and chopped
1 eggplant, trimmed and cubed
1 orange bell pepper, seeded and chopped
One 14-oz can chopped tomatoes
⅔ cup lamb or vegetable broth
Salt and freshly ground black pepper
¾ cup bulgur wheat
¼ cup raisins
3 Tbsp pine nuts
1 Tbsp grated lemon zest

TO GARNISH
2 Tbsp chopped fresh cilantro

ITALIAN LAMB WITH PASTA

ORIGINALLY GROWN IN EUROPE, FENNEL IS A BULBOUS LEAF STALK OFTEN REFERRED
TO AS FLORENCE FENNEL. IT CAN BE EATEN RAW OR COOKED AND HAS A TASTE SIMILAR TO ANISE.

Cover the dried mushrooms in almost boiling water
for 20 minutes, then drain, reserving the soaking liquor.

Heat 1 tablespoon of the oil in the open cooker and brown
the lamb shanks on all sides (this can be done in batches).
Remove from the cooker and add the remaining oil. Sauté
the garlic, sundried tomatoes, onion, fennel, and all the
mushrooms for 5 minutes or until the onion has softened.
Remove from the cooker and set aside. Pour in the puréed
tomatoes and red wine and stir well to remove any sediment
sticking to the base.

Place the trivet rim-side down into the cooker and place
the lamb shanks on top. Arrange the onion-and-mushroom
mixture over the lamb and add the chopped oregano and
seasoning to taste. Close the lid and bring to 15 lb pressure
and cook for 20 minutes.

Depressurize quickly and remove the lid. Remove the lamb
and vegetables and keep warm. Place the pasta in the
foil-lined separator with $2^{1}/_{2}$ cups boiling water, cover
with foil, and secure with fine twine. Place on the trivet.
Close the lid and return to pressure. Cook for 5 minutes
then depressurize quickly.

Drain the pasta and serve with the lamb, vegetables,
and sauce on a warmed serving platter, garnished with
fresh oregano sprigs.

Serves **4**
Cook control **15 lb**
Preparation time **10 minutes**
Open cooking time **10 minutes**
Pressure cooking time
   25 minutes

¼ cup dried mushrooms
2 Tbsp oil
Two 8-oz lamb shanks
4 garlic cloves, peeled
   and crushed
1 oz sundried tomatoes, chopped

1 medium onion, peeled and cut
   into wedges
1 head fennel, trimmed and sliced
1½ cups button mushrooms,
   wiped
1¼ cups puréed tomatoes
1¼ cups red wine
1 Tbsp chopped fresh oregano
Salt and freshly ground
   black pepper
8 oz dried pasta shapes

TO GARNISH
Fresh oregano sprigs

HERB MEAT LOAF

YOU CAN USE GROUND BEEF, LAMB, PORK, OR CHICKEN FOR THIS DISH, BUT BUY THE BEST QUALITY YOU CAN AFFORD. CHEAPER GROUND MEAT CONTAINS A LOT OF FAT AND YOU WILL END UP WITH A MUCH SMALLER LOAF.

Place the ground beef, sausage meat, onion, garlic, herbs, and bread crumbs into a mixing bowl and mix well.
Blend the tomato paste and horseradish sauce with seasoning and add to the mixture, then add the egg and sufficient brandy to bind the mixture together.

Place in a 4-cup ovenproof container and press down lightly. Cover with a double layer of waxed paper.

Place the trivet in the cooker rim-side down and add $2\frac{1}{2}$ cups water and 2 tablespoons lemon juice. Place the container on top of the trivet and close the lid. Bring to 15 lb pressure and cook for 20 minutes. Depressurize quickly, remove the waxed paper and serve immediately, garnished with fresh herbs, with gravy and freshly cooked vegetables.

Serves **8**
Cook control **15 lb**
Preparation time **10 minutes**
Pressure cooking time
   20 minutes

1 lb ground beef
4 oz sausage meat
1 medium onion, peeled and
   chopped fine
2 garlic cloves, peeled
   and crushed
2 Tbsp chopped fresh mixed herbs
¾ cup fresh white bread crumbs

2 Tbsp tomato paste
1 Tbsp hot horseradish sauce
Salt and freshly ground
   black pepper
1 medium egg
2 to 3 Tbsp brandy
2 Tbsp lemon juice

TO GARNISH
Fresh herb sprigs

TO SERVE
Gravy and freshly cooked
   vegetables

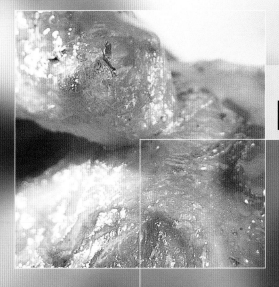

POULTRY

CHICKEN CHASSEUR

IF A WINE IS NOT WORTH DRINKING, IT IS RARELY WORTH COOKING WITH.
TRY TO USE GOOD WINE FOR COOKING, OR YOU MAY SPOIL THE FINISHED DISH.

Heat the oil in the open cooker and sauté the onions and bacon until lightly browned. Remove. Seal the chicken portions on all sides in the oil remaining in the cooker then remove from the cooker and drain off any excess oil.

Return the onions, bacon, and chicken to the pan and add the mushrooms and tomatoes. Blend the tomato paste with the wine and broth then pour over the chicken. Close the lid and bring to 15 lb pressure and cook for 5 minutes.

Depressurize quickly, lift out the chicken and vegetables, and keep warm. Blend the flour and butter together to form a paste. Bring the liquid in the pan to a boil then whisk small amounts of the flour paste into the boiling liquid. Cook until smooth and thickened. Add seasoning to taste then pour the sauce over the chicken and onions, sprinkle with parsley, and serve with mashed potatoes and either a green salad or freshly cooked vegetables.

Serves **4**
Cook control **15 lb**
Preparation time **12 minutes**
Open cooking time **5 minutes**
Pressure cooking time **5 minutes**

2 Tbsp oil
8 baby onions, peeled
4 slices bacon, chopped
4 boneless, skinless chicken portions
3 cups large field mushrooms, wiped and sliced
8 cherry tomatoes, halved
2 Tbsp tomato paste
1¼ cups red wine
⅔ cup chicken broth
1 Tbsp white all-purpose flour
1 Tbsp softened butter
Salt and freshly ground black pepper

TO GARNISH
1 Tbsp chopped fresh parsley

TO SERVE
Mashed potatoes, and green salad or vegetables

COQ AU VIN

THIS CLASSIC FRENCH DISH WORKS PERFECTLY WHEN COOKED IN THE PRESSURE COOKER. FOR A MORE INTENSE FLAVOR, MARINATE THE CHICKEN PORTIONS IN THE RED WINE AND BRANDY FOR 2 TO 3 HOURS BEFORE COOKING.

Heat the oil in the open cooker and brown the chicken portions on all sides. Remove from the cooker and reserve. Add the shallots, garlic, and bacon to the cooker and sauté for 3 minutes then add the mushrooms and continue to sauté for 1 minute.

Return the chicken portions to the cooker and pour in the red wine, broth, and seasoning to taste.

Close the lid and bring to 15 lb pressure and cook for 5 minutes. Depressurize quickly and remove the lid. Pour over the brandy and stir.

Place the trivet in the cooker rim-side down. Place the potatoes in the separator and place on top of the trivet and close the lid.

Return to 15 lb pressure and cook for 4 minutes then depressurize quickly. Remove the lid and separator and place the potatoes in a serving dish, and keep warm. Remove the chicken from the cooker with the shallots and mushrooms, place on a warmed serving dish, and keep warm.

Blend the butter and flour together to form a smooth paste then bring the liquid in the cooker to a boil and whisk in small spoonfuls of the paste. Continue to whisk until the sauce is smooth and thickened. Adjust seasoning to taste, stir in the crème fraîche or sour cream with the parsley, pour over the chicken and shallots, and serve.

Serves **4**
Cook control **15 lb**
Preparation time **10 minutes**
Open cooking time **10 minutes**
Pressure cooking time **9 minutes**

1 Tbsp oil
Four 6-oz chicken quarters
8 shallots, peeled
4 to 6 garlic cloves, peeled and
  sliced
8 slices bacon, cut into small dice
1½ cups button mushrooms, wiped
1¼ cups red wine
⅔ cup chicken broth
Salt and freshly ground
  black pepper
3 Tbsp brandy
12 oz baby new potatoes, scrubbed
1 Tbsp softened butter
1 Tbsp white all-purpose flour
2 Tbsp crème fraîche or sour cream
1 Tbsp chopped fresh parsley

ALMOND AND PECAN-STUFFED
CHICKEN BREASTS

THIS DELICIOUS RECIPE COMBINES THE CLASSIC FLAVORS OF CITRUS AND FRESH HERBS WITH
CHICKEN AND NUTS FOR A HEALTHY YET FILLING DISH.

Wipe the chicken breasts and, using a sharp knife, slit along the longest edge of each chicken breast to form a pocket. Wipe with paper towels and set aside.

Mix together the scallions, ground almonds, bread crumbs, pecans, lemon zest, tarragon, and seasoning and bind together with the beaten egg and sufficient orange juice to make a moist but not wet stuffing. Use to stuff the cavities in the chicken breasts. Press the edges firmly together.

Melt the butter with the oil in the open cooker then brown the chicken on all sides. Pour in the remaining orange juice with the honey and close the lid. Bring to 15 lb pressure and cook for 5 minutes. Depressurize quickly then lift out the chicken and keep warm. Strain the cooking juices into a cleaned pan and bring to a boil. Blend the cornstarch with 1 tablespoon water and add to the boiling liquor. Cook, stirring until slightly thickened. Pour over the chicken and garnish with the tarragon sprigs and orange wedges. Serve with green salad or freshly cooked vegetables and new potatoes or noodles.

Serves **4**
Cook control **15 lb**
Preparation time **10 minutes**
Open cooking time **5 minutes**
Pressure cooking time **5 minutes**

4 boneless, skinless
chicken breasts
6 scallions, trimmed and chopped
½ cup ground almonds
½ cup fresh white bread crumbs
½ cup pecans, chopped
1 Tbsp grated lemon zest
1 Tbsp chopped fresh tarragon
Salt and freshly ground
black pepper

1 medium egg, beaten
1¼ cups orange juice
1 Tbsp butter
1 Tbsp oil
2 tsp honey
1 Tbsp cornstarch

TO GARNISH
Fresh tarragon sprigs and
orange wedges

TO SERVE
Green salad or freshly cooked
vegetables, and new potatoes
or noodles

TURKEY WITH TARRAGON

TARRAGON IS AN HERB THAT GOES PARTICULARLY WELL WITH BOTH POULTRY AND FISH.

Serves **4**
Cook control **15 lb**
Preparation time **5 minutes**
Open cooking time
 5 to 6 minutes
Pressure cooking time
 7 minutes

2 Tbsp oil
1 lb boneless, skinless turkey
 thigh, diced
2 medium onions, peeled
 and sliced
1 head fennel, trimmed
 and sliced
2 large carrots, peeled and
 cut into half moons

⅔ cup dry white wine
1¼ cups turkey or chicken broth
2 Tbsp chopped fresh tarragon
1 Tbsp grated orange zest
Salt and freshly ground
 black pepper
1 Tbsp cornstarch

TO GARNISH
Orange zest, orange wedges,
 and tarragon sprigs

TO SERVE
New potatoes, sugar snap peas,
 and broccoli

Heat one tablespoon of the oil in the open cooker and seal the diced turkey on all sides. Using a slotted spoon remove the turkey from the cooker and reserve. Add the remaining oil to the cooker and sauté the onion, fennel, and carrot for 5 minutes.

Return the turkey to the cooker then add the wine, broth, tarragon, and orange zest with seasoning to taste. Close the lid, bring to 15 lb pressure. Cook for 7 minutes and depressurize quickly. Remove the turkey and vegetables from the cooker with a slotted spoon and keep warm.

Bring the liquor remaining in the cooker to a boil. Blend the cornstarch with one tablespoon water, stir into the boiling liquid and cook, stirring until thickened. Adjust the seasoning, pour the sauce over the turkey, garnish, and serve.

CILANTRO CHICKEN

THIS DISH OFFERS A SPICY FLAVOR, WHICH IS TEMPERED BY THE SMOOTH COCONUT MILK.

Serves **4**
Cook control **15 lb**
Preparation time **10 minutes**
Open cooking time **8 minutes**
Pressure cooking time
 10 minutes

2 Tbsp oil
Four 8-oz chicken portions,
 thoroughly defrosted if frozen
1 medium onion, peeled and
 cut into wedges
4 garlic cloves, peeled and
 chopped
1 Tbsp mild curry paste

4 medium tomatoes, skinned,
 seeded and chopped
1¼ cups coconut milk
⅔ cup chicken broth
10 oz sweet potatoes,
 peeled and diced
1 green bell pepper, seeded
 and chopped
8 oz green beans, trimmed
 and halved
Salt
1 tsp paprika
1 Tbsp cornstarch
2 Tbsp chopped fresh cilantro

Heat 1 tablespoon of the oil in the open cooker and brown the chicken portions on all sides. Remove from the cooker and set aside. Add the remaining oil then the onion and garlic to the cooker and sauté for 1 minute then add the curry paste and cook, stirring for 2 minutes. Add the chopped tomatoes, coconut milk, broth, diced sweet potato, and the reserved chicken and close the lid. Bring to 15 lb pressure and cook for 8 minutes then depressurize quickly.

Remove the lid and add the green bell pepper and beans, close the lid, and return to 15 lb pressure. Cook for 2 minutes then depressurize quickly and remove the chicken portions.

Add salt and paprika to taste then blend the cornstarch with 1 tablespoon of water and stir into the cooker. Cook, stirring until the sauce thickens then stir in the chopped cilantro, pour over the chicken, and serve.

CHICKEN WITH OKRA
AND FENNEL TAGINE

OKRA, ALSO KNOWN AS LADIES' FINGERS, IS AN ANNUAL PLANT OF THE COTTON FAMILY AND NATIVE TO AFRICA. WELL KNOWN IN CREOLE COOKING, IT IS USED WHEN MAKING GUMBO.

Heat 1 tablespoon of the oil in the open cooker and sauté the chicken for 5 minutes until well-sealed and golden brown. Using a slotted spoon, remove from the cooker and reserve.

Add the remaining oil to the cooker and sauté the onion, garlic, ginger, chile, and fennel for 2 minutes. Return the chicken to the cooker with the saffron, tomatoes, zucchini, okra, apricots, and cinnamon sticks.

Pour in the broth, add seasoning to taste, then close the lid and bring to 15 lb pressure. Cook for 3 minutes then depressurize quickly. Discard the cinnamon sticks and serve garnished with the olives and parsley and either freshly cooked cinnamon-flavored bulgur wheat, couscous or potatoes, and salad.

Serves **4**
Cook control **15 lb**
Preparation time **15 minutes**
Open cooking time **8 minutes**
Pressure cooking time **3 minutes**

2 Tbsp oil
1 lb diced fresh boneless, skinless chicken
1 medium onion, peeled and sliced
3 garlic cloves, peeled and sliced
1 small piece gingerroot, peeled and grated
1 small jalapeño chile, seeded and chopped
1 head fennel, trimmed and chopped
A few strands saffron
3 medium tomatoes, seeded and chopped

1 large zucchini, trimmed and chopped
8 oz okra, trimmed and chopped in half if large
¾ cup dried apricots, chopped
2 cinnamon sticks, bruised
1¼ cups chicken broth
Salt and freshly ground black pepper

TO GARNISH
A few black olives and flat-leaf parsley

TO SERVE
Cinnamon-flavored bulgur wheat, couscous or potatoes, and salad

ROCK CORNISH HENS
WITH KUMQUATS

KUMQUATS ARE TINY, SLIGHTLY BITTER-TASTING ORANGES THAT ARE EATEN WHOLE.
IF THEY ARE UNAVAILABLE, SUBSTITUTE WITH 1 TO 2 ORDINARY ORANGES OR BLOOD ORANGES.

Halve the rock Cornish hens, rinse, and pat dry. Heat the oil in the open cooker and seal the hens on all sides. Remove from the cooker and wipe the cooker clean.

Return the hens to the cooker with the unpeeled garlic cloves, bay leaves, broth, and orange juice. Sprinkle in the orange zest, vinegar, and sugar with the soy sauce and add the tarragon with a little seasoning. Cut the kumquats in half, add to the cooker, and close the lid.

Bring to 15 lb pressure and cook for 10 minutes. Depressurize quickly then remove the rock Cornish hens and kumquats from the cooker and place on a warmed serving plate. Strain the liquid, return to the cooker and bring to a boil. Blend the cornstarch with one tablespoon water and stir into the boiling liquid. Cook, stirring until the sauce thickens. Adjust the seasoning, garnish the rock Cornish hens, and serve with the sauce and freshly cooked vegetables.

Serves **4**
Cook control **15 lb**
Preparation time **5 minutes**
Open cooking time **5 minutes**
Pressure cooking time
 10 minutes

2 large rock Cornish hens
2 Tbsp oil
10 unpeeled garlic cloves
2 bay leaves
1¼ cups chicken broth
⅔ cups orange juice
1 Tbsp grated orange zest
2 Tbsp white wine vinegar
1 Tbsp light brown sugar
2 Tbsp dark soy sauce
1 Tbsp chopped fresh tarragon
Salt and freshly ground black
 pepper
12 kumquats
1 Tbsp cornstarch

TO GARNISH
Fresh tarragon sprigs and extra
 kumquats

TO SERVE
Freshly cooked vegetables

CAJUN TURKEY

TURKEY HAS THE LOWEST FAT CONTENT OF ALL MEAT AND POULTRY AND IS THEREFORE IDEAL FOR PEOPLE WHO ARE WATCHING THEIR CALORIE INTAKE. ANOTHER BONUS IS THAT IT COMBINES WELL WITH MANY DIVERSE FLAVORS.

Trim the turkey, dice, place in a shallow dish then scatter over the chopped onion, garlic, dried crushed chiles, and cardamom pods. Blend the spices and lemon zest with the light corn syrup, ketchup, and lemon juice, mix well, then pour over the turkey. Cover loosely and allow to marinate in the refrigerator for at least 30 minutes, overnight if time permits. Stir the turkey occasionally during this time.

When ready to cook, heat the oil in the open cooker and seal the turkey on all sides. Stir half the marinade into 1¼ cups of the broth then pour over the turkey.

Place the trivet rim-side down on top of the turkey and line the separator with foil. Place the pasta into the separator and pour over the remaining broth. Cover with a double sheet of waxed paper.

Close the lid and bring to 15 lb pressure and cook for 5 minutes. Depressurize quickly then remove the pasta and drain if necessary.

Blend the cornstarch with 1 tablespoon water and stir into the cooker. Bring to a boil and cook, stirring until the sauce has thickened. Stir the chopped cilantro into the pasta and serve with the cooked turkey.

Serves **4**
Cook control **15 lb**
Preparation time **15 minutes**
  plus 30 minutes marinating time
Open cooking time **3 minutes**
Pressure cooking time **5 minutes**

1 lb fresh turkey breast meat
1 medium onion, peeled and chopped
4 garlic cloves, peeled and crushed
½ to 1 tsp dried crushed chiles
5 cardamom pods, bruised
1 tsp ground coriander
½ tsp pumpkin pie spice
1 tsp paprika
1 Tbsp grated lemon zest
2 tsp light corn syrup, warmed
4 Tbsp ketchup
2 Tbsp lemon juice
1 Tbsp oil
3 cups turkey or chicken broth, hot
6 oz dried pasta shapes
1 Tbsp cornstarch
2 Tbsp chopped fresh cilantro

APRICOT AND CRANBERRY-
STUFFED TURKEY

SMALL TURKEY JOINTS MAKE AN EXCELLENT MEAL AND ARE QUICKLY COOKED
WHEN USING THE PRESSURE COOKER.

Wipe the turkey joint and make two deep pockets along each length of the joint. Set aside.

Heat one tablespoon of the oil in the open cooker and sauté the shallots, garlic, and mushrooms for 5 minutes. Place into a bowl and wipe the cooker clean.

Add the apricots, cranberry sauce, orange zest, bread crumbs, parsley, and seasoning to taste to the shallots and mix to a stiff consistency with the egg and orange juice. Use to stuff the pockets in the turkey. Pinch the edges together and if liked bind with fine twine.

Heat the remaining oil in the cooker and seal the joint on all sides and then cover with the bacon. Pour in the broth, wine, and add the red currant jelly. Close the lid and bring to 15 lb pressure. Cook for 15 minutes. Depressurize quickly and remove the joint from the cooker. Keep warm.

Bring the liquor in the cooker to a boil and cook, stirring until the sauce thickens then strain into a serving jug. Garnish the joint and serve with the sauce and freshly cooked vegetables.

Serves **4 to 6**
Cook control **15 lb**
Preparation time **10 minutes**
Open cooking time **5 minutes**
Pressure cooking time
  15 minutes

1 whole turkey breast fillet joint
2 Tbsp oil
4 shallots, peeled and chopped
2 garlic cloves, peeled and
  crushed
1¼ cups button mushrooms,
  wiped and chopped
¾ cup dried apricots, chopped
2 Tbsp cranberry sauce
1 Tbsp grated orange zest
1 cup fresh white bread crumbs

2 Tbsp chopped fresh parsley
Salt and freshly ground black
  pepper
1 medium egg, beaten
1 to 2 Tbsp orange juice
8 to 10 slices bacon
⅔ cup turkey or chicken broth
1¼ cups rosé or white wine
1 Tbsp red currant jelly

TO GARNISH
Fresh cranberries and fresh
  apricots

TO SERVE
Freshly cooked potatoes
  and vegetables

ROCK CORNISH HENS
WITH RED CABBAGE

THE RED CABBAGE AND APPLE ARE A PERFECT FOIL FOR THE ROCK CORNISH HENS IN THIS DISH.

Wipe the rock Cornish hens joints then heat the the oil in the open cooker and brown the joints on all sides (this takes about 5 minutes). Remove from the cooker and wipe the cooker clean.

Thoroughly rinse the red cabbage in cold water and drain well. Place in a bowl with the chopped onion, apple, sugar, dill, and seasoning to taste. Mix well and pour over the balsamic vinegar.

Place the joints in the cooker and pour over the broth. Put the trivet in the cooker rim-side down and place the red cabbage on the trivet. Close the lid and bring to 15 lb pressure. Cook for 10 minutes then depressurize quickly. Remove the joints and cabbage from the cooker and keep warm.

Blend the butter and flour together to form a paste. Bring the liquid remaining in the cooker to a boil then whisk in small spoonfuls of the flour paste. Continue to whisk until the sauce has thickened and is smooth. Serve with the rock Cornish hen joints, the red cabbage, and mashed potatoes. Garnish with dill sprigs.

Serves **4**
Cook control **15 lb**
Preparation time **15 minutes**
Open cooking time **5 minutes**
Pressure cooking time
   10 minutes

4 small or 2 large rock Cornish hens, jointed or use guinea fowl
1 Tbsp oil
1 small red cabbage (about 1½ lb in weight) trimmed and shredded
1 onion, peeled and chopped
1 large tart cooking apple, peeled, cored, and chopped

1 Tbsp dark brown sugar
2 Tbsp chopped fresh dill
Salt and freshly ground black pepper
1 Tbsp balsamic vinegar
1¼ cups chicken broth
1 Tbsp softened butter
1 Tbsp white all-purpose flour

TO GARNISH
Dill sprigs

TO SERVE
Mashed potatoes

ROCK CORNISH HENS WITH
CANNELLINI BEANS AND OLIVE

THIS IS THE KIND OF DISH THAT APPEALS TO MEN, AS IT IS MEATY, FULL OF FLAVOR, AND THERE'S PLENTY OF IT!

Cover the beans in boiling water and soak for 1 hour. Drain and reserve. Cut the rock Cornish hens into joints, rinse, and dry well on paper towels.

Heat 1 tablespoon of the oil and seal the joints all over then remove from the cooker and set aside. Add the remaining oil, onion, and garlic and sauté for 3 minutes then add the mushrooms and continue to sauté for 1 minute.

Return the beans to the cooker and place the joints on top. Pour over the red wine and broth with the honey and add a little seasoning with all but 1 tablespoon of the olives.

Close the lid, bring to 15 lb pressure and cook for 10 minutes.

Depressurize quickly and remove the joints from the cooker. Keep warm. Drain off the liquid from the beans and arrange the beans round the pheasant and return the liquid to the cooker.

Blend the butter and flour together to form a smooth paste. Bring the liquid in the cooker to a gentle boil then whisk in small spoonfuls of the flour paste. Cook, whisking until the sauce thickens and is smooth. Adjust the seasoning, add the remaining black olives and the chopped parsley, and pour over the joints. Serve with mashed potatoes and freshly cooked green vegetables.

Serves **4**
Cook control **15 lb**
Preparation time **10 minutes**
  plus **1 hour soaking time**
Open cooking time **9 minutes**
Pressure cooking time
  10 minutes

1 cup dried cannellini beans
2 large rock Cornish hens
  (about 2½ lb total weight)
2 Tbsp oil
1 medium onion, peeled and sliced
3 garlic cloves, peeled and
  chopped

3 cups closed-cup mushrooms,
  wiped and chopped
⅔ cup red wine
1¼ cups chicken broth
2 tsp honey
Salt and freshly ground black
  pepper
¾ cup pitted black olives
1 Tbsp softened butter
1 Tbsp white all-purpose flour
2 Tbsp chopped fresh parsley

TO SERVE
Mashed potatoes and freshly
  cooked green vegetables

CARIBBEAN CHICKEN

YAMS FEATURE PROMINENTLY IN WEST INDIAN COOKING AND ARE COOKED LIKE POTATOES.

Heat the oil in the open cooker and seal the chicken portions on all sides, remove from the cooker, and reserve. Add the garlic, chile, and yam to the oil in the cooker and sauté in the open cooker for 5 minutes. Add the bell peppers and cook for 2 minutes. Remove the vegetables from the pan and clean.

Return the chicken and yam mixture to the cooker with the chopped mango, brown sugar, juice, broth, and soy sauce. Add seasoning, close the lid, and bring to 15 lb pressure. Cook for 10 minutes. Depressurize quickly then remove the chicken and yam, straining off the liquid, and place on a warm serving platter. Keep warm. Bring the cooking liquid to a boil in the open cooker and add the cilantro. Blend the cornstarch with one tablespoon water then stir into the boiling liquid. Cook, stirring until thickened. Season and pour over the chicken. Garnish with mango and cilantro.

Serves **4**
Cook control **15 lb**
Preparation time **10 minutes**
Open cooking time **12 minutes**
Pressure cooking time
  10 minutes

2 Tbsp oil
4 skinless chicken portions
4 garlic cloves, peeled and
  chopped in half
1 green serrano chile, seeded
  and chopped
1 large yam, peeled and cubed
1 red bell pepper, seeded
  and sliced

1 yellow bell pepper, seeded
  and sliced
1 almost ripe mango, peeled,
  pitted, and chopped
2 tsp brown sugar
⅔ cup mango or orange juice
1¼ cups chicken broth
2 Tbsp dark soy sauce
Salt and freshly ground black
  pepper
2 Tbsp chopped fresh cilantro
1 Tbsp cornstarch

TO GARNISH
Extra chopped mango and cilantro

SPICED CHICKEN WITH
CRANBERRIES AND ORANGE

THERE IS SOMETHING VERY EVOCATIVE ABOUT THE FRAGRANCE OF CRANBERRIES COOKING, PERHAPS BECAUSE THEY ARE ASSOCIATED WITH CHILDHOOD AND CHRISTMAS.

Dice the chicken thighs then heat one tablespoon of the oil in the open cooker and seal the chicken on all sides. Using a slotted spoon remove the chicken from the cooker. Add the remaining oil to the cooker then sauté the shallots and celery for 5 minutes or until beginning to soften.

Return the chicken to the cooker then add the rosemary sprigs, cranberries, orange zest, cinnamon stick, orange juice, and broth with seasoning. Close the lid and bring to 15 lb pressure and cook for 3 minutes. Depressurize quickly then place the trivet on top.

Line the separator with foil and place the pasta in the separator with 2¹/₂ cups boiling water. Place on the trivet and close the lid. Return to pressure and cook for 5 minutes. Depressurize quickly then remove the separator and drain the pasta. Serve the chicken on top of the pasta, garnished with the rosemary sprigs, cranberries, and orange wedges.

Serves **4**
Cook control **15 lb**
Preparation time **5 minutes**
Open cooking time **10 minutes**
Pressure cooking time **8 minutes**

8 skinless, boneless chicken
  thighs
2 Tbsp oil
8 shallots, peeled and cut into
  wedges
4 celery stalks, trimmed and cut
  into chunks
2 small sprigs fresh rosemary

1 cup fresh or defrosted frozen
  cranberries
1 long strip thin pared
  orange zest
1 cinnamon stick, bruised
4 Tbsp orange juice
²/₃ cup chicken broth
Salt and freshly ground black
  pepper
8 oz pasta shapes

TO GARNISH
Rosemary sprigs, cranberries,
  and orange wedges

DUCK WITH FIGS AND PORT

I PREFER TO EAT MY DUCK BREASTS SLIGHTLY PINK BUT IF YOU LIKE YOUR DUCK WELL-DONE, JUST COOK FOR AN EXTRA 1 TO 2 MINUTES.

Wipe the duck breasts and make 3 diagonal slashes across each. Heat the oil in the open cooker then seal the duck breasts on all sides. Remove from the cooker with a slotted spoon and drain on paper towels.

Add the shallots to the oil remaining in the cooker and sauté for 3 minutes then drain off any excess oil and add the chopped dried figs.

Return the duck breasts to the cooker and pour in the orange juice, broth, and port, seasoning to taste.

Close the lid and bring to 15 lb pressure. Cook for 12 to 15 minutes (depending on whether you like your duck medium-rare or well-done). Depressurize quickly and remove the duck from the cooker and keep warm. Place the shallots and figs with the liquid into a blender and blend to form a purée. Return to the cooker, stir in the cream, and heat gently. Adjust the seasoning then pour over the duck breasts and serve, garnished with fresh figs and parsley, with freshly cooked vegetables.

Serves **4**
Cook control **15 lb**
Preparation time **5 minutes**
Open cooking time **8 minutes**
Pressure cooking time
  12 to 15 minutes

4 boneless duck breasts
1 Tbsp oil
4 shallots, peeled and cut
  into wedges
½ cup ready-to eat dried figs,
  chopped

⅔ cup orange juice
⅔ cup chicken broth
3 Tbsp port
Salt and freshly ground black
  pepper
4 Tbsp light cream

TO GARNISH
Fresh figs and flat-leaf parsley

TO SERVE
Freshly cooked vegetables

LEMON-BRAISED CHICKEN
WITH CUMIN

THIS CHICKEN DISH IS PERFECT FOR A SPRING DAY, WHEN YOU WANT A SLIGHTLY MORE SUBSTANTIAL
MEAL THAN SALAD. THIS VERSION, USING SCALLION IN THE MASHED POTATOES, IS A REAL WINNER.

Cut the chicken into bite-size pieces and reserve. Heat the oil in the open cooker and brown the chicken on all sides. Using a slotted spoon remove the chicken from the cooker and set aside.

Add the onion to the cooker and sauté for 2 minutes. Add the lemon, cumin seeds, and ground coriander and sauté for 1 minute. Return the chicken to the cooker. Pour in the white wine, ⅔ cup water, the honey, and a little seasoning.

Place the trivet rim-side down in the cooker and place the separator on top. Place the potatoes in the separator and close the lid. Bring to 15 lb pressure and cook for 3 minutes.

Depressurize quickly then remove the potatoes from the cooker and place in a bowl. Add seasoning to taste with the butter and mash until smooth. Add the cream or yogurt with the scallions and mix well. Keep warm.

Blend the cornstarch with 2 tablespoons water and stir into the chicken and liquor left in the cooker. Cook over a gentle heat, stirring until thickened. Adjust the seasoning then serve with the scallion-flavored mashed potatoes and a green salad.

Serves **4**
Cook control **15 lb**
Preparation time **10 minutes**
Open cooking time **8 minutes**
Pressure cooking time **3 minutes**

1¼ lb skinless boneless chicken
1 Tbsp oil
1 medium onion, peeled, sliced, and cut into half-moon shapes
1 small lemon, sliced, and cut into half-moon shapes
1 tsp cumin seeds
½ tsp ground coriander
⅔ cup medium dry white wine

2 tsp honey
Salt and freshly ground black pepper
1½ lb potatoes, peeled and cut into chunks
2 Tbsp butter
2 Tbsp light cream or low-fat, plain yogurt
4-5 scallions, trimmed, and chopped
1 Tbsp cornstarch

TO SERVE

Salad

BLACK-EYED PEAS
AND CHICKEN CASSEROLE

BONELESS CHICKEN THIGH MEAT WORKS VERY WELL IN THIS RECIPE. THE SLIGHTLY MORE GAMEY FLAVOR OF THE THIGH MEAT COMPLEMENTS THE PEAS.

Cover the dried peas with boiling water, soak for 1 hour, then drain. Place the peas in the open cooker with 2¹/₂ cups cold water and bring to a boil. Remove any scum that floats to the surface then reduce the heat slightly. Close the lid, and maintaining the same heat, bring to 15 lb pressure. Cook for 5 minutes then depressurize slowly.

Discard the cooking liquid and reserve the peas. Wipe the cooker clean and heat the oil in the open cooker and seal the bacon and chicken all over.

Add the onion, fennel, and carrots and continue to cook for 3 minutes, stirring frequently.

Add the contents of the can of tomatoes and return the peas to the cooker. Add seasoning to taste, the Cajun seasoning, oregano, and broth and stir lightly. Arrange the sliced sweet potatoes on top and close the lid.

Bring to 15 lb pressure and cook for 5 minutes then depressurize slowly. Remove the lid and arrange the chicken, peas, and sweet potatoes in a warm dish, sprinkle with the herbs, and serve with crusty bread.

Serves **6**
Cook control **15 lb**
Preparation time **10 minutes**
  plus 1 hour soaking time
Open cooking time **6 minutes**
Pressure cooking time
  10 minutes

1 cup dried black-eyed peas
1 Tbsp oil
8 slices bacon, diced
1 lb boneless, skinless chicken
  portions, diced
1 medium onion, peeled and
  chopped
1 head fennel, trimmed and diced
2 medium carrots, peeled and
  diced
One 14-oz can chopped tomatoes
Salt and freshly ground
  black pepper
1 tsp Cajun seasoning
2 Tbsp chopped fresh oregano
1¼ cups chicken broth
12 oz sweet potatoes, peeled
  and sliced
1 Tbsp chopped fresh oregano
  or parsley

TO SERVE
Crusty bread

ASPARAGUS AND BELL PEPPER
TURKEY ROULADE

THIS DISH IS ONE OF MY ALL-TIME FAVORITES. ALTHOUGH IT IS A LITTLE ELABORATE TO ASSEMBLE,
IT IS WELL WORTH THE EFFORT.

Place the turkey steaks between 2 sheets of waxed paper and pound with a meat mallet until $1/4$ inch thick. Place on a chopping board and set aside.

Blanch 12 to 16 asparagus spears in boiling water for 5 minutes, drain, and pat dry. Place 3 to 4 asparagus spears (depending on size) and 2 to 3 strips of red bell pepper on each turkey steak and roll up. Wrap two slices of Parma ham round each roll and secure with fine twine.

Heat the oil in the open cooker and brown the rolls on all sides. Place the trivet rim-side down on top of the roulades and place the remaining asparagus, bell pepper strips, and onion wedges on top. Pour over the broth, wine, honey, and soy sauce. Bring to 15 lb pressure and cook for 5 minutes. Depressurize quickly and remove the roulades and vegetables from the cooker. Keep warm.

Beat the butter and flour together to form a paste. Bring the liquid in the open cooker to a boil then whisk small spoonfuls of the flour paste into the boiling liquid. Cook, stirring for 3 to 4 minutes until the sauce is thickened and glossy.

Serve, garnished with the parsley, with cooked vegetables, new potatoes, and the sauce.

Serves **4**
Cook control **15 lb**
Preparation time **15 minutes**
Open cooking time **8 minutes**
Pressure cooking time **5 minutes**

4 thin turkey breast steaks
12 oz baby asparagus spears, trimmed
2 red bell peppers, seeded and sliced
8 thin slices Parma ham
1 Tbsp oil
1 orange bell pepper, seeded, skinned, and sliced
1 medium onion, peeled and cut into wedges

1¼ cups turkey or chicken broth
⅔ cup dry white wine
2 tsp honey
2 Tbsp dark soy sauce
1 Tbsp softened butter
1 Tbsp white all-purpose flour
Salt and freshly ground black pepper

TO GARNISH
Flat-leaf parsley

TO SERVE
Cooked vegetables, and new potatoes

JAMAICAN SPICED TURKEY

IF YOUR TURKEY JOINT IS LARGER THAN 2 LB OR IS QUITE TALL IN SHAPE SO THAT THE SEPARATOR
WILL NOT SIT IN THE COOKER LEVEL, THEN COOK THE RICE SEPARATELY.

Wipe the turkey joint, make 3 to 4 slashes across the top, then place in a shallow dish.
Blend the hot chili sauce, crushed garlic, allspice, rum, ketchup, and oil together.
Pour or brush over the joint, cover loosely, and allow to marinate in the refrigerator
for at least 30 minutes, longer if time permits. Brush or spoon the marinade over the joint
occasionally during marinating.

Place the trivet rim-side down in the cooker and brush lightly with a little oil then pour
in the fruit juice and broth. Drain the turkey joint and place on the trivet. Close the lid
and bring to 15 lb pressure. Cook for 20 minutes then depressurize quickly.

Meanwhile line the separator with foil and add the rice. Stir the chopped chile into the rice
then pour over the hot broth. Cover with a double sheet of waxed paper. Place on top of the
joint and close the lid. Return to 15 lb pressure and cook for 5 minutes. Depressurize
slowly and remove the rice and turkey from the cooker.

Fluff up the rice with a fork and stir in the chopped cilantro and place with the turkey onto
a warmed serving dish and garnish with cilantro sprigs and mango slices.

Serves **6**
Cook control **15 lb**
Preparation time **5 minutes plus**
  30 minutes marinating time
Pressure cooking time
  25 minutes

One 2-lb boneless turkey joint
2 Tbsp hot chili sauce
4 garlic cloves, peeled and crushed
1 tsp allspice
2 Tbsp dark rum
4 Tbsp ketchup
2 Tbsp oil
1 cup mango or orange juice
1 cup turkey or chicken broth, warmed
1 cup long-grain rice
1 red jalapeño chile
2 cups vegetable broth
1 Tbsp chopped fresh cilantro

TO GARNISH
Cilantro sprigs and mango slices

VEGETABLES

BUTTERNUT SQUASH CASSEROLE

BUTTERNUT SQUASH IS NATIVE TO TROPICAL AMERICA, BUT NOW GROWS IN NORTH AMERICA
AS WELL. IT CAN BE BOILED, STEWED, OR STUFFED AND BAKED.

Heat the oil in the open cooker and sauté the onion, garlic, chile, and butternut squash for 3 minutes. Add the sweet potatoes, sliced bell pepper, and sugar and sauté for 1 minute.

Add the chopped tomatoes with their juice, the broth or water, and the Worcestershire sauce and close the lid. Bring to 15 lb pressure and cook for 3 minutes.

Depressurize quickly then add seasoning to taste and sprinkle with the chopped parsley before serving.

Serves **4**
Cook control **15 lb**
Preparation time **15 minutes**
Open cooking time **4 minutes**
Pressure cooking time **3 minutes**

1 Tbsp oil
1 medium onion, peeled and
   cut into wedges
3 to 5 garlic cloves, peeled
   and sliced
1 serrano chile, seeded and sliced
1 small butternut squash (about
   1 lb in weight), peeled and diced

8 oz sweet potatoes, peeled
   and diced
1 red bell pepper, seeded
   and sliced
1 green bell pepper, seeded
   and sliced
1 tsp dark brown sugar
One 14-oz can chopped tomatoes
1 cup vegetable broth or water
1 Tbsp Worcestershire sauce
Salt and freshly ground
   black pepper

TO GARNISH
Chopped fresh parsley

WINTER VEGETABLE STEW

THIS IS A WARM AND HEARTY MEAL THAT IS IDEAL TO SERVE AS A MAIN COURSE WITH WARM WHOLE-GRAIN BREAD.

Place the pot barley in the open cooker and add 4 cups water. Close the lid and bring to 15 lb pressure. Cook for 18 minutes. Depressurize slowly then remove the pot barley from the cooker, drain, and set aside. Wipe the cooker clean.

Add the oil to the open cooker and sauté the onion, garlic, parsnips, celery, carrots, and potatoes for 2 minutes. Return the pot barley to the cooker with the contents of the can of tomatoes, the broth, seasoning, and chopped oregano. Close the lid and bring to 15 lb pressure. Cook for 3 minutes then depressurize quickly.

Line the separator with foil and place the cabbage in the separator. Add 6 tablespoons hot water and sprinkle with the caraway seeds. Place the trivet rim-side down on top of the vegetables in the cooker and place the separator on top of the trivet. Close the lid and bring to 15 lb pressure. Cook for 1 minute then depressurize quickly.

Remove the separator from the cooker and add seasoning to taste to the cabbage. Remove the trivet, adjust the seasoning, and serve with the cabbage and chunks of warm whole-grain bread.

Serves **6**
Cook control **15 lb**
Preparation time **15 minutes**
Open cooking time **2 minutes**
Pressure cooking time
  22 minutes

½ **cup pot barley**
1 **Tbsp oil**
1 **large onion, peeled and cut**
  into wedges
4 **garlic cloves, peeled**
  and chopped
2 **parsnips, peeled and cut**
  into wedges
3 **celery stalks, trimmed**
  and chopped

2 **carrots, about 6 oz in weight,**
  trimmed, peeled, and sliced
10 **oz potatoes, peeled and**
  cut into chunks
One 14-oz can chopped tomatoes
⅔ **cup vegetable broth**
Salt and freshly ground
  black pepper
1 **Tbsp chopped fresh oregano**
1 **lb green cabbage, trimmed**
  and shredded
1 **tsp caraway seeds**

TO SERVE
Warm whole-grain bread

MAPLE-GLAZED BABY ROOT
VEGETABLES

MAPLE SYRUP IS A FAVORITE FOR EVERYONE WITH A SWEET TOOTH, AND GOES WELL WITH PANCAKES
AND DESSERTS OR, AS IN THIS RECIPE, TO FLAVOR VEGETABLES.

Serves **4 to 6**
Cook control **15 lb**
Preparation time **15 minutes**
Open cooking time **8 to 9 minutes**
Pressure cooking time **4 minutes**

8 baby onions, peeled

8 oz baby turnips, peeled

8 oz baby carrots, trimmed and peeled or scrubbed

8 oz baby new potatoes, scrubbed

8 oz baby parsnips, trimmed and peeled

1 Tbsp oil

1 tsp brown sugar

2 Tbsp maple syrup

1 tsp chili sauce, or to taste

1¼ cups vegetable broth

1 Tbsp chopped fresh thyme

Salt and freshly ground black pepper

TO GARNISH

Fresh thyme sprigs

Cut all the vegetables in halves or quarters if necessary so they are all of a similar size. Heat the oil in the open cooker and sauté all the vegetables for 5 minutes. Add the sugar, maple syrup, and chili sauce and stir well.

Pour in the liquid then add the chopped thyme and close the lid. Bring to 15 lb pressure and cook for 4 minutes. Depressurize quickly then drain, reserving the liquid. Add seasoning to taste to the vegetables, place in a serving dish, and keep warm.

Boil the liquid in the cooker for 3 to 4 minutes or until syrupy then pour over the vegetables and serve garnished with the thyme sprigs.

CORN ON THE COB WITH
HERB AND GARLIC BUTTER

CORN ON THE COB IS DELICIOUS COOKED ON THE BARBECUE. IF YOU ARE IN A HURRY, COOK THEM IN THE PRESSURE COOKER WHILE WAITING FOR THE BARBECUE TO HEAT UP, THEN FINISH THEM ON THE BARBECUE.

Serves **4**
Cook control **15 lb**
Preparation time **5 to 8 minutes**
Pressure cooking time **10 minutes**

¾ stick butter, softened

2 garlic cloves, peeled and crushed

1 Tbsp grated lemon zest

1 Tbsp chopped fresh parsley

1 Tbsp chopped fresh thyme

1 Tbsp snipped fresh chives

4 whole corn on the cob

Cream the butter until very soft then beat in the crushed garlic, lemon zest, and chopped herbs. Shape into a roll, wrap in waxed paper, and chill in the refrigerator for 30 minutes or until firm.

Remove and discard the outer leaves and silky threads from the corn on the cob and rinse well.

Place in the cooker and pour in 1¼ cups water. Close the lid and bring to 15 lb pressure. Cook for 10 minutes then depressurize quickly. Remove the corn on the cobs and place a large piece of herb and garlic butter on top to serve.

FRAGRANT NEW POTATOES
WITH SHALLOTS

A MORTAR AND PESTLE IS AN INVALUABLE KITCHEN TOOL BECAUSE IT ENABLES SPICE
PODS TO BE LIGHTLY CRACKED OPEN WITHOUT LOSING THE SEEDS INSIDE THE PODS.

Heat the oil in the open cooker and sauté the lemon grass, coriander seeds, grated ginger, and garlic for 2 minutes. Add the potatoes and shallots and continue to sauté for 3 minutes.

Add the coconut milk, soy sauce, and broth then close the lid. Bring to 15 lb pressure and cook for 4 minutes.

Depressurize quickly and drain. Discard the lemon grass stalks. Add seasoning to taste, together with the cilantro and serve.

Serves **4**
Cook control **15 lb**
Preparation time **10 minutes**
Open cooking time **5 minutes**
Pressure cooking time **4 minutes**

1 Tbsp oil
2 lemon grass stalks (outer leaves discarded), lightly crushed
1 tsp coriander seeds, crushed
1 small piece gingerroot, peeled and grated fine
2 garlic cloves, peeled and crushed
1 lb baby new potatoes, scrubbed
8 oz shallots, peeled
⅔ cup coconut milk
1 Tbsp light soy sauce
⅔ cup vegetable broth, heated to boiling point
Salt and freshly ground black pepper
2 Tbsp fresh cilantro leaves

POTATO DAUPHINOIS

WHEN PREPARING THIS RECIPE, ENSURE THAT THE DISH YOU WISH TO USE FITS INSIDE THE PRESSURE COOKER AND THAT IT IS OVENPROOF SO YOU CAN BROWN THE CHEESE AT THE END OF COOKING UNDER THE BROILER.

Butter a round ovenproof 5-cup dish. Slice the sweet potatoes fairly thick then rinse the sweet and ordinary potatoes in cold water and pat dry with paper towels. Place a layer of both potatoes, the onions and garlic in the dish and pour over a little of the cream. Sprinkle with some of the grated Monterey Jack or cheddar cheese and a little Parmesan cheese.

Repeat the layering until all the potatoes are used up, ending with a layer of cream and cheese. Cover with a double layer of waxed paper and secure.

Pour 2¹⁄₂ cups of water into the cooker and place the trivet rim-side down in the cooker. Place the dish on the trivet and close the lid. Bring to 15 lb pressure and cook for 20 minutes. Depressurize quickly then remove the dish and discard the paper. Preheat the broiler then cook the potatoes under the broiler for 4 to 5 minutes, turning the dish occasionally until the top is golden.
Serve immediately.

Serves **3 to 4**
Cook control **15 lb**
Preparation time **15 minutes**
Pressure cooking time
  20 minutes

1 tsp melted butter
6 oz sweet potatoes, peeled
10 oz potatoes, peeled and
  sliced thin
1 small onion, peeled and
  sliced thin
2 to 4 garlic cloves, peeled
  and crushed
²⁄₃ cup heavy cream
1 cup grated Monterey Jack or
  Cheddar cheese
2 Tbsp Parmesan cheese, grated

CREOLE OKRA STEW

WHEN USING CHILES REMEMBER THAT THE HEAT IS NOT ONLY IN THE SEEDS BUT ALSO IN THE MEMBRANE TO WHICH THE SEEDS ARE ATTACHED. ALWAYS WASH YOUR HANDS WELL AFTER HANDLING CHILES.

Serves **3 to 4**
Cook control **15 lb**
Preparation time **10 minutes**
Open cooking time **5 minutes**
Pressure cooking time **2 minutes**

1 Tbsp oil
4 garlic cloves, peeled and sliced
1 to 2 green serrano chiles, seeded and chopped
1 medium onion, peeled and sliced
4 celery stalks, trimmed and chopped
1 large red bell pepper, seeded and chopped
4 oz green beans, trimmed and halved
8 oz okra, trimmed
1 tsp allspice
1 Tbsp chopped fresh oregano
4 medium tomatoes, (about 10 oz) chopped
⅔ cup vegetable broth, heated to boiling
Salt and freshly ground black pepper

TO GARNISH
Oregano sprigs

Heat the oil in the open cooker and sauté the garlic, chiles, onion, and celery for 3 minutes. Add the red bell pepper, beans, and okra then sprinkle in the allspice. Sauté for 2 minutes then add the oregano and tomatoes. Pour over the boiling broth.

Close the lid and bring to 15 lb pressure. Cook for 3 minutes then depressurize quickly. Drain then add seasoning to taste and serve garnished with oregano sprigs.

RED CABBAGE WITH
APPLE AND CARAWAY

COOKED RED CABBAGE TAKES ON A WONDERFULLY DEEP RICH PURPLE-RED COLOR. COUPLED WITH ITS DELICIOUS TASTE, THIS IS ONE VEGETABLE THAT SHOULD BE PART OF ANY COOK'S REPERTOIRE.

Serves **4 to 6**
Cook control **15 lb**
Preparation time **8 minutes**
Pressure cooking time
  4 minutes

1 red cabbage, about 2 lb
  in weight
1 small onion, peeled and
  sliced thin

1 tart cooking apple, peeled,
  cored, and sliced
2 Tbsp dark brown sugar
3 Tbsp cider vinegar
1 tsp caraway seeds
Salt and freshly ground
  black pepper
2 cups vegetable broth or water
1 Tbsp chopped fresh parsley

Discard any outer leaves and stalk from the cabbage and shred fine. Wash thoroughly in plenty of cold water and drain. Place in the open cooker. Add the onion, sliced apple, sugar, vinegar, caraway seeds, and seasoning to taste then stir lightly. Pour over the broth and close the lid.

Bring to 15 lb pressure and cook for 4 minutes. Depressurize quickly then drain off the excess liquid and serve sprinkled with the chopped parsley.

FENNEL SUPPER

FENNEL SEEMS TO BE ONE OF THOSE VEGETABLES THAT MANY PEOPLE ARE NOT QUITE SURE WHAT TO DO WITH. HERE, I HAVE COMBINED IT WITH LEEKS, CARROTS, GARLIC, AND POTATOES TO CREATE A TASTY SUPPER DISH. THE BACON IS OPTIONAL, BUT CERTAINLY COMPLEMENTS THE FLAVOR OF THE DISH.

Serves **4**
Cook control **15 lb**
Preparation time **10 minutes**
Open cooking time **2 minutes**
Pressure cooking time
   3 minutes

1 Tbsp oil
3 garlic cloves, trimmed
   and sliced
12 slices bacon, chopped,
   optional
2 heads fennel, trimmed
   and sliced
2 leeks, about 10 oz in weight,
   trimmed and sliced thick
10 oz new potatoes, scrubbed
   and sliced thick
2 large carrots, about 8 oz in
   weight, trimmed, peeled,
   and sliced
Salt and freshly ground
   black pepper
½ tsp grated fresh nutmeg
2 Tbsp chopped fresh tarragon
1¼ cups vegetable broth

TO SERVE
Freshly grated Monterey Jack
   or sharp cheddar cheese

Heat the oil then sauté the garlic and bacon, if using, for 2 minutes. Remove the garlic and bacon and set aside.

Arrange the fennel, leeks, new potatoes, and carrots in layers sprinkling with a little of the garlic, and bacon if used. Season each layer with salt, pepper, nutmeg, and a little of the chopped tarragon. When all the vegetables have been used, pour over the broth and close the lid.

Bring to 15 lbs pressure and cook for 3 minutes then depressurize quickly and serve with grated cheese.

THAI VEGETABLES

BIRD'S EYE CHILES ARE VERY HOT INDEED. USE SPARINGLY UNLESS YOU KNOW THAT YOU CAN TAKE THE HEAT. WEAR RUBBER GLOVES WHEN HANDLING.

Serves **4**
Cook control **15 lb**
Preparation time **15 minutes**
Open cooking time **3 minutes**
Pressure cooking time
   1 minute

1 Tbsp oil
2 to 3 garlic cloves, peeled
   and crushed
2 lemon grass stalks (outer
   leaves discarded), bruised
1 small piece fresh gingerroot,
   peeled and grated fine
1 to 2 bird's eye or green jalapeño
   chiles, seeded and chopped
1 cinnamon stick, bruised
6 oz broccoli florets
6 oz cauliflower florets
2 carrots, peeled and chopped
1 large zucchini, trimmed and
   cut into thick slices
4 oz green beans, trimmed
   and halved
⅔ cup coconut milk
Salt and freshly ground
   black pepper
1 Tbsp chopped fresh cilantro

Heat the oil in the open cooker and sauté the garlic, lemon grass, ginger, chiles, and cinnamon stick for 2 minutes. Add the vegetables and sauté for 1 minute.

Pour in the coconut milk with ⅔ cup boiling water then close the lid and bring to 15 lb pressure. Cook for 1 minute then depressurize quickly and discard the lemon grass and cinnamon. Season and serve sprinkled with the chopped cilantro.

(For really crisp vegetables, bring to pressure then remove from the heat and depressurize quickly—for soft vegetables, pressure cook for 2 minutes.)

FAVA BEAN AND BACON SUCCOTASH

FRESH FAVA BEANS ARE ONLY IN SEASON FOR A VERY SHORT TIME SO MAKE GOOD USE OF THEM WHEN THEY ARE AVAILABLE. OTHERWISE, USE FROZEN BEANS.

Heat the oil in the open cooker and sauté the onions, garlic, chile, and bacon for 2 minutes. Add the fava beans and corn. Blend the tomato paste with the broth and pour over the vegetables.

Close the lid and bring to 15 lb pressure. Cook for 2 minutes then depressurize quickly and add seasoning to taste. Drain the fava bean mixture and place in a serving bowl. Keep warm.

Bring the cooking liquid in the open cooker to a boil. Blend the cornstarch with 1 tablespoon water to form a smooth paste then stir into the boiling liquid. Cook, stirring until slightly thickened and smooth. Pour over the fava bean mixture and serve sprinkled with the scallions and the Parmesan cheese.

Serves **3 to 4**
Cook control **15 lb**
Preparation time **10 minutes**
Open cooking time **5 minutes**
Pressure cooking time **2 minutes**

1 Tbsp oil
3 baby onions, peeled and cut into thin wedges
2 to 3 garlic cloves, peeled and sliced
1 jalapeño chile, seeded and sliced
12 slices bacon, derinded and chopped
2 cups fava beans, preferably fresh shelled
1 cup corn kernels
1 Tbsp tomato paste
1¼ cups vegetable broth, heated to almost boiling
Salt and freshly ground black pepper
2 tsp cornstarch
6 scallions, trimmed and diagonally sliced

TO SERVE
Grated or shaved Parmesan cheese

RATATOUILLE

THIS RATATOUILLE IS SUBSTANTIAL ENOUGH TO BE SERVED AS A MAIN COURSE WITH PLENTY OF WARM CRUSTY BREAD OR NEW POTATOES, AND PARMESAN CHEESE.

Heat the oil in the open cooker then sauté the eggplant, onion, fennel, squash, dried chiles, and garlic for 3 minutes. Add the red and yellow bell peppers and the tomatoes and sauté for 1 minute.

Blend the tomato paste with the red wine then stir in the tomato juice and pour over the vegetables. Close the lid and bring to 15 lb pressure. Cook for 2 minutes then depressurize quickly.

Remove the lid and add seasoning to taste, stir in the shredded basil, and serve with shavings of Parmesan cheese.

Serves **6**
Cook control **15 lb**
Preparation time **15 minutes**
Open cooking time **4 minutes**
Pressure cooking time **2 minutes**

3 Tbsp olive oil
1 eggplant, about 12 oz in weight, trimmed and diced
1 medium onion, peeled and cut into wedges
1 head fennel, trimmed and sliced
2 acorn squash, peeled, seeded, and chopped
½ to 1 tsp crushed dried chiles

4 garlic cloves, peeled and chopped
1 red bell pepper, seeded and cut into chunks
1 yellow bell pepper, seeded and cut into chunks
10 oz ripe tomatoes, chopped
2 Tbsp tomato paste
⅔ cup red wine
⅔ cup tomato juice
Salt and freshly ground black pepper
2 Tbsp shredded basil

TO SERVE
Shavings of Parmesan cheese

DRIED BEANS, PASTA, AND CEREALS

GREEN RICE

DIFFERENT TEXTURES ARE TO MY MIND AN INTEGRAL PART IN THE ENJOYMENT OF A MEAL. HERE THE
RAW INGREDIENTS ARE ADDED AT THE END OF THE COOKING TIME, GIVING THIS DISH ITS CRUNCH.
IF PREFERRED, HOWEVER, THEY CAN BE ADDED TO THE REST OF THE INGREDIENTS AND COOKED.

Serves **4**
Cook control **10 lb**
Preparation time **5 minutes**
Pressure cooking time **2 minutes**

1 cup premixed wild and long-grain rice
1 green jalapeño chile, seeded and chopped
2 garlic cloves, peeled and crushed
1 green bell pepper, seeded and chopped
1 cup fresh shelled peas
8 scallions, trimmed and chopped
¾ cup pitted olives, chopped
Salt and freshly ground black pepper
2 Tbsp chopped fresh cilantro

Place the rice in the open cooker and add 7½ cups of water. Close the lid and bring to 10 lb pressure. Cook for 2 minutes then depressurize slowly.

Add the chile, garlic, half the green bell pepper, and peas. Stir well then close the lid. Return to 10 lb pressure then remove from the heat and depressurize slowly.

Drain the rice thoroughly and place in a bowl and stir in the remaining chopped bell pepper, the scallions, chopped olives, and seasoning to taste. Mix lightly then sprinkle with the chopped cilantro and serve.

BROWN RICE SALAD

THIS SALAD HAS A DISTINCT ORIENTAL FLAVOR. LOOK OUT FOR SEASONED RICE VINEGAR IN YOUR LOCAL ORIENTAL OR HEALTH FOOD STORE.

Serves **6**
Cook control **15 lb**
Preparation time **12 minutes**
Open cooking time **4 minutes**
Pressure cooking time **4 minutes**

1¼ cups brown rice
1 tsp tumeric
Salt and freshly ground black pepper
2 Tbsp oil
2 garlic cloves, peeled and chopped
1 yellow bell pepper, seeded and chopped
½ cup carrot, peeled and shredded
8 oz asparagus, trimmed and cut into small pieces
8 scallions, trimmed and chopped
½ cup canned water chestnuts, drained and sliced
2 Tbsp light soy sauce
3 Tbsp seasoned rice vinegar
2 Tbsp chopped fresh cilantro
2 Tbsp toasted sesame seeds

Place the rice in the open cooker and add 7½ cups of water, tumeric, and salt to taste. Close the lid and bring to 15 lb pressure. Cook for 4 minutes then depressurize slowly, drain the rice, and set aside. Wipe the cooker clean.

Heat the oil in the open cooker and sauté the garlic, bell pepper, carrot, and asparagus for 4 minutes or until the vegetables are tender but still crisp. Return the rice to the cooker and stir in the remaining ingredients except for the sesame seeds. Stir well then turn into a serving dish, sprinkle with the sesame seeds and serve.

CHILE BEAN POT

WHEN COOKING MORE THAN ONE TYPE OF BEAN IN THE PRESSURE COOKER
MAKE SURE THEY REQUIRE THE SAME AMOUNT OF COOKING TIME.

Soak both kinds of dried beans in boiling water for 1 hour, drain, and set aside.

Heat the oil in the open cooker and sauté the onion, garlic, and chiles for 3 minutes.
Add the tomatoes, fava beans, and thyme then add the drained beans.

Blend the tomato paste with 2 cups of the broth and pour into the cooker, then bring to
a boil. Close the lid and bring to 15 lb pressure. Cook for 7 minutes. Depressurize slowly
then stir in the mushrooms.

Line the separator with foil and place the rice into the separator. Pour over the remaining
broth, cover with foil, and secure.

Place the trivet rim side down over the beans and place the rice on top. Close the lid and
bring to 15 lb pressure. Cook for 5 minutes. Depressurize slowly. Remove the rice from the
cooker and arrange in a warm serving dish. Season the beans then spoon over the rice
and garnish with the parsley.

Serves **4 to 6**
Cook control **15 lb**
Preparation time **10 minutes plus**
  1 hour soaking time
Open cooking time **3 minutes**
Pressure cooking time
  12 minutes

1 cup dried red kidney beans
1 cup dried flageolet beans
1 Tbsp oil
1 medium onion, peeled and sliced
3 to 4 garlic cloves, peeled and sliced
2 to 3 serrano chiles, seeded and sliced
8 oz tomatoes, peeled and chopped
¾ cup shelled fava beans
1 Tbsp chopped fresh thyme
1 Tbsp tomato paste
4 cups vegetable broth
1½ cups closed-cup mushrooms,
  wiped and chopped thick
1 cup long-grain rice
Salt and freshly ground black pepper

TO GARNISH
2 Tbsp chopped fresh parsley

BEAN SALAD WITH PECAN DRESSING

TO MIX THE PECANS WELL INTO THE DRESSING, PROCESS THEM WITH ALL THE HERBS IN A BLENDER UNTIL CHOPPED FINE, OR ALTERNATIVELY, CHOP THE BEANS AND HERBS TOGETHER BY HAND ON A CHOPPING BOARD.

Place the beans together in a large bowl and cover with plenty of boiling water, leave for 1 hour, then drain and place in the open cooker with 4 cups cold water.

Close the lid and bring to 15 lb pressure. Cook for 10 minutes then depressurize slowly then drain the beans and place in a large bowl.

Add the chopped scallions, celery, shredded carrot, and halved cherry tomatoes then mix lightly together.

Place the olive oil, orange juice, seasoning, the garlic, orange zest, chopped herbs, and pecans in a screw-top jar and shake vigorously until blended. Pour over the bean mixture and mix until the beans are lightly coated. Serve.

Serves **6 to 8**
Cook control **15 lb**
Preparation time **12 minutes**
   plus 1 hour soaking
Pressure cooking time
   10 minutes

¾ **cup dried borlotti beans**
¾ **cup dried red kidney or black-eyed peas**
¾ **cup dried cannellini beans**
8 scallions, trimmed and chopped
3 celery stalks, trimmed and chopped fine
2 medium carrots, trimmed and shredded
1 cup cherry tomatoes, quartered
6 Tbsp olive oil
4 Tbsp orange juice
Salt and freshly ground black pepper
2 garlic cloves, peeled and crushed
1 Tbsp grated orange zest
2 Tbsp chopped fresh cilantro
1 Tbsp chopped fresh flat-leaf parsley
½ **cup pecans, chopped fine**

WILD MUSHROOM RISOTTO

IT IS IMPORTANT WHEN USING DRIED MUSHROOMS THAT YOU REHYDRATE THEM FULLY BEFORE USE.
DO MAKE SURE THAT YOUR WATER IS NOT BOILING WHEN YOU POUR IT OVER THE MUSHROOMS
AND LEAVE FOR AT LEAST 20 MINUTES.

Place the dried mushrooms in a small bowl and cover with almost-boiling water, soak for 20 minutes, then drain, reserving the liquid and mushrooms.

Place the rice in the open cooker and add 7½ cups cold water. Close the lid and bring to 15 lb pressure. Cook for 2 minutes then depressurize slowly, drain the rice, and reserve. Wipe the cooker clean.

Heat the oil in the open cooker then sauté the garlic, chile, and onion for 3 minutes. Add the red and yellow bell pepper and wild mushrooms and sauté for 1 minute. Stir in the rehydrated mushrooms and the button mushrooms with the rice. Blend the tomato paste with the reserved mushroom soaking liquid then pour into the cooker with the vegetable broth. Close the lid and bring to 15 lb pressure. Depressurize slowly then add seasoning to taste and the chopped parsley, stir well, and serve with the shavings of Parmesan cheese.

Serves **4**
Cook control **15 lb**
Preparation time **10 minutes**
  plus 20 minutes soaking time
Open cooking time **4 minutes**
Pressure cooking time **2 minutes**

¼ **cup dried porcini mushrooms (ceps)**
1 cup long-grain rice
1 Tbsp oil
6 garlic cloves, peeled and chopped
2 red jalapeño chiles, seeded and chopped
1 medium onion, peeled and chopped
1 red bell pepper, seeded and chopped

1 yellow bell pepper, seeded and chopped
4½ cups assorted wild mushrooms, wiped and sliced if large
1½ cups button mushrooms, wiped and sliced
2 Tbsp tomato paste
½ **cup vegetable broth**
Salt and freshly ground black pepper
2 Tbsp chopped fresh flat-leaf parsley

TO SERVE
Shavings of Parmesan cheese

BULGUR PILAU

IF YOU CANNOT FIND WHOLE CINNAMON STICKS, USE 1 TO 1½ TEASPOONS GROUND CINNAMON.

Heat the oil in the open cooker and sauté the garlic, onion, eggplant, and cinnamon stick for 3 minutes. Add the red bell pepper, orange zest, and half the cherry tomatoes and pour over 1¼ cups of the orange juice and water. Place the trivet rim-side down on top of the vegetables.

Line the separator with foil and add the bulgur wheat. Pour in the remaining orange juice and water, cover with foil, and secure. Place on the trivet.

Close the lid and bring to 15 lb pressure. Cook for 5 minutes then depressurize slowly.

Remove the separator from the cooker and place the bulgur wheat in a bowl. Stir with a fork to fluff up. Drain the vegetables then stir into the bulgur wheat with the remaining tomatoes, paprika, seasoning to taste, and the almonds. Stir lightly, sprinkle with the chopped cilantro, and serve.

Serves **4**
Cook control **15 lb**
Preparation time **15 minutes**
Open cooking time **3 minutes**
Pressure cooking time **5 minutes**

2 Tbsp olive oil
3 to 4 garlic cloves, peeled and crushed
1 medium onion, peeled and chopped
1 medium eggplant, about 12 oz in weight, trimmed and diced
1 cinnamon stick, bruised
1 red bell pepper, seeded and chopped
1 Tbsp grated orange zest
8 oz cherry tomatoes
2½ cups orange juice and water mixed
1¼ cups bulgur wheat
1 tsp paprika
Salt and freshly ground black pepper
2 Tbsp toasted flaked almonds
1 Tbsp chopped fresh cilantro

PASTA WITH FRUIT AND BEANS

COOKING PASTA IN ORANGE JUICE MAY SOUND STRANGE, BUT DO TRY IT. I GUARANTEE YOU'LL LOVE IT.

Soak the dried beans in boiling water for 1 hour then drain and place in the open cooker. Add 2½ cups water and bring to a boil. Skim off any scum that floats to the surface, reduce the heat under the cooker to a gentle boil, and close the lid. Bring to 15 lb pressure and cook for 10 minutes. Depressurize slowly then drain the beans and set aside.

Rinse the cooker then heat the oil in the open cooker and sauté the onion, fennel, and dried apricots for 2 minutes. Add the raisins, one of the apples, and the orange zest, then pour over 1¼ cups of the orange juice and water. Place the trivet, rim-side down, on top.

Line the separator with tin foil and add the pasta. Pour over the remaining orange juice and water.

Close the lid and bring to 15 lb pressure. Cook for 2 minutes.

Depressurize slowly then strain the pasta if necessary and place in a bowl. Add the fennel and apricot mixture, the remaining diced apple, chopped scallions, the reserved red kidney beans, seasoning to taste, and the chopped cilantro. Mix lightly together and serve with the grated cheese.

Serves **3 to 4**
Cook control **15 lb**
Preparation time **10 minutes**
  plus 1 hour soaking time
Open cooking time **2 minutes**
Pressure cooking time **2 minutes**

¾ cup dried red kidney beans
1 Tbsp olive oil
1 medium onion, peeled and chopped
1 head fennel, about 8 oz in weight, trimmed and chopped
¾ cup dried apricots, chopped
½ cup raisins
2 apples, peeled, cored, and diced
1 Tbsp grated orange zest
3 cups orange juice and water mixed
6 oz dried pasta shapes
6 scallions, trimmed and sliced
Salt and freshly ground black pepper
2 Tbsp chopped fresh cilantro

TO SERVE
Grated cheese, such as cheddar or Monterey Jack

PUY LENTIL AND RICE PILAF

PUY LENTILS VARY IN SIZE AND ARE HIGHLY REGARDED BY MANY TO BE THE BEST LENTIL. LIKE GREEN AND CONTINENTAL LENTILS, THEY RETAIN THEIR SHAPE WHEN COOKED.

Cover the Puy lentils with boiling water, soak for 10 minutes, then drain.

Heat the oil in the open cooker and sauté the garlic and onion for 3 minutes. Add the carrots and green bell pepper and continue to sauté for 2 minutes.

Add the drained Puy lentils with the cinnamon stick, oregano, and tomatoes and stir well. Pour over ²/₃ cup of the broth. Place the trivet rim-side down in the cooker.

Line the separator with foil and add the rice. Pour in the remaining broth. Cover with foil and secure. Place on the trivet and close the lid.

Bring to 15 lb pressure and cook for 3 minutes. Depressurize slowly then remove the separator and fluff the rice with a fork to separate the grains.

Season the Puy lentil mixture, discard the cinnamon stick, then mix in the cooked rice and serve garnished with the oregano.

Serves **4**
Cook control **15 lb**
Preparation time **10 minutes**
   plus 10 minutes soaking time
Open cooking time **5 minutes**
Pressure cooking time **3 minutes**

¾ cup Puy lentils
1 Tbsp olive oil
4 garlic cloves, peeled and crushed
1 medium onion, peeled and chopped
2 medium carrots, peeled and cut into large chunks
1 green bell pepper, seeded and chopped
1 cinnamon stick, bruised
1 Tbsp chopped fresh oregano
4 medium tomatoes, chopped
1¼ cups vegetable broth
¾ cup basmati rice
Salt and freshly ground black pepper

TO GARNISH
Chopped fresh oregano

SPICED PASTA

SPICES MUST BE AS FRESH AS POSSIBLE TO PROVIDE MAXIMUM FLAVOR. IT IS BEST TO GRIND SPICES MANUALLY WITH A MORTAR AND PESTLE AS YOU NEED THEM, BUT IF THIS IS NOT POSSIBLE STORE YOUR SPICES IN A COOL DARK CUPBOARD SO THEY RETAIN AS MUCH FLAVOR AS POSSIBLE. BUY IN SMALL QUANTITIES SO YOU USE THEM QUICKLY.

Heat the oil in the open cooker and sauté the garlic, onion, fennel, and chiles for 3 minutes then sprinkle in the spices with seasoning to taste and cook for 1 minute. Add 1¼ cups of the broth. Place the trivet rim-side down in the cooker.

Line the separator with foil and add the pasta, pour in the remaining broth, and cover with a double sheet of waxed paper. Place on top of the trivet.

Close the lid and bring to 15 lb pressure and cook for 2 minutes. Depressurize quickly and drain the pasta and add to the cooker with the artichoke hearts, green beans, and sugar snap peas. Close the lid and return to 15 lb pressure. Depressurize slowly, adjust the seasoning, stir in the chopped cilantro, and serve.

Serves **4**
Cook control **15 lb**
Preparation time **10 minutes**
Open cooking time **4 minutes**
Pressure cooking time **2 minutes**

1 Tbsp oil
4 garlic cloves, peeled and
  chopped
1 medium onion, peeled and
  sliced fine
1 head fennel, trimmed and
  chopped
1 to 2 green serrano chiles,
  seeded and chopped

1 tsp ground coriander
1 tsp ground cumin
1 tsp ground ginger
Salt and freshly ground black
  pepper
3 cups vegetable broth
6 oz dried pasta shapes
One 14-oz can artichoke hearts,
  drained and sliced
4 oz green beans, trimmed
  and halved
4 oz sugar snap peas, trimmed
1 Tbsp chopped fresh cilantro

VEGETABLE COUSCOUS

THESE DAYS IT IS VERY EASY TO FIND INSTANT COUSCOUS. FLUFF IT UP WELL BEFORE SERVING.

Heat the oil in the open cooker and sauté the garlic, onion, sundried tomatoes, and eggplant for 2 minutes. Add the remaining fresh vegetables and stir. Add the tomatoes and their juice with ⅔ cup of the broth, seasoning, and 1 tablespoon of the chopped basil. Stir lightly. Place the trivet rim-side down on top of the vegetables.

Line the separator with foil and add the couscous, and pour over the remaining broth. Cover with foil and secure. Stand on the trivet and close the lid. Bring the cooker to 15 lb pressure and cook for 3 minutes. Depressurize slowly then remove the couscous from the cooker and turn into a bowl. Add the remaining basil and butter and fork up until fluffy. Arrange the vegetables on a warmed serving platter, garnish with the basil, and serve with the couscous.

Serves **4**
Cook control **15 lb**
Preparation time **15 minutes**
Open cooking time **2 minutes**
Pressure cooking time **3 minutes**

2 Tbsp olive oil

3 to 4 garlic cloves, peeled and crushed

1 red onion, peeled and cut into wedges

2 Tbsp sundried tomatoes, chopped

1 medium eggplant, trimmed and diced

1 red bell pepper, seeded and chopped into large pieces

1 yellow bell pepper, seeded and chopped into large pieces

2 medium zucchini, trimmed and diced into large chunks

One 14-oz can chopped tomatoes

1¼ cups vegetable broth, almost boiling

Salt and freshly ground black pepper

2 Tbsp chopped fresh basil

1¼ cups couscous

3 Tbsp softened butter

TO GARNISH
Shredded basil sprigs

BROWN RICE WITH BASIL

THIS DISH MAKES A GOOD VEGETARIAN MAIN COURSE AS WELL AS AN
EXCELLENT ACCOMPANIMENT TO STEAK OR CHOPS.

Place the rice in the open cooker and add 7$\frac{1}{2}$ cups of water and salt to taste. Close the lid and bring to 15 lb pressure. Cook for 4 minutes then depressurize slowly, drain the rice, and reserve. Wipe the cooker clean.

Heat the oil in the open cooker and sauté the leeks, garlic, and mushrooms for 2 minutes. Add the tomatoes and broccoli and pour over the broth. Close the lid and return to 15 lb pressure and cook for 2 minutes. Depressurize quickly then drain off any excess broth and spoon into a bowl and mix in the cooked rice. Blend the olive oil, lemon zest, and juice together, add seasoning to taste and the basil then pour over the rice, stir lightly, then serve.

Serves **6**
Cook control **15 lb**
Preparation time **15 minutes**
Open cooking time **2 minutes**
Pressure cooking time **6 minutes**

1¼ cups brown rice
Salt and freshly ground black
   pepper
2 Tbsp oil
2 large leeks, trimmed and sliced
4 garlic cloves, peeled and
   chopped

3 cups baby button mushrooms,
   wiped
4 medium tomatoes, seeded
   and chopped
6 oz broccoli, broken into small
   florets
1¼ cups vegetable broth
3 Tbsp olive oil
1 Tbsp grated lemon zest
2 Tbsp lemon juice
2 Tbsp chopped fresh basil

HUMMUS

A MIDDLE EASTERN DISH THAT HAS PROVED TO BE VERY POPULAR IN THE WEST EITHER AS A DELICIOUS SNACKING TYPE FOOD OR AS A HEALTHY AND NUTRITIOUS STARTER.

Cover the garbanzos with boiling water and soak for 1 hour. Drain and place in the cooker with 4 cups cold water. Bring to a boil and remove any scum from the surface with a slotted spoon. Add the garlic, lemon zest, ground cumin, and chili powder. Reduce the heat slightly then close the lid and bring to 15 lb pressure. Cook for 20 minutes.

Depressurize slowly then drain the garbanzos and place in a food processor. Add the lemon juice and tahini paste and blend to a coarse purée. With the motor still running, slowly pour in sufficient olive oil to give a smooth purée. Add seasoning to taste.

Scrape into a small serving bowl, sprinkle with the toasted pine nuts and paprika, and serve with strips of warm pita bread.

Serves **8**
Cook control **15 lb**
Preparation time **10 minutes plus**
   1 hour soaking time
Pressure cooking time
   20 minutes

1 cup dried garbanzos
4 to 6 garlic cloves, peeled
1-1½ Tbsp grated lemon zest
1 tsp ground cumin
1 tsp mild chili powder
3 Tbsp lemon juice
2 to 3 Tbsp tahini paste
About 1¼ cups olive oil
Salt and freshly ground black pepper

TO GARNISH
2 Tbsp toasted pine nuts and paprika

TO SERVE
Strips of warm pita bread

DESSERTS
AND PRESERVES

CHOCOLATE STEAMED PUDDINGS

THIS IS AN ELEGANT DESSERT TO SERVE AT A DINNER PARTY.

Lightly oil and line the bases of four individual pudding bowls or ramekins. (Ensure they will all fit into the cooker.) Stir the chocolate to ensure there are no lumps and allow to cool.

Cream the butter and sugar together then gradually beat in the eggs, adding a little flour after each addition. When all the eggs have been added, stir in the melted chocolate and then the remaining flour. Stir well then divide between the four bowls and level the top. Cover each with a double sheet of waxed paper or oiled sheet of foil with a pleat in the center and secure firmly with twine.

Place the trivet rim-side down in the cooker and pour 4 cups boiling water and a little lemon juice into the cooker. Place the puddings on the trivet. Close the lid and presteam for 5 minutes.

Bring the cooker to 15lb pressure and cook for 7 minutes then release the steam slowly for about 10 minutes. Unmold and serve dusted with confectioner's sugar, berries, and a sauce of your choice. (If using foil add an extra 3 minutes to the cooking time.)

Serves **4**
Cook control **15 lb**
Preparation time **10 to 15 minutes**
Presteaming time **5 minutes**
Pressure cooking time **7 minutes**

2 oz semisweet chocolate, melted
1 stick sweet butter
½ cup light brown sugar
2 small eggs, beaten
1 cup self-rising flour

TO SERVE
Confectioner's sugar, fresh summer
  berries, and chocolate or red
  fruit sauce

STICKY TOFFEE PUDDING

THIS STICKY TOFFEE PUDDING IS A PERFECT, COMFORTING DESSERT TO SERVE ON A COLD DAY.

Oil a 4-cup mixing bowl or six individual pudding bowls or ramekins and place a small circle of oiled waxed paper in the base. Set aside.

Cream the butter and sugar together then gradually beat in the eggs with a little of the flour. When all the eggs have been added stir in the light corn syrup followed by the remaining flour, the dates, and the pecans.

Turn into the prepared bowl, ensuring that the bowl is only filled two-thirds full. Cover with a double sheet of waxed paper and secure firmly with fine twine.

Place the trivet rim-side down in the cooker and stand the bowl on top of the trivet.

Pour in 4 cups boiling water with a little lemon juice. Close the lid and presteam for 15 minutes. Bring to 10 lb pressure and cook for 25 to 30 minutes.

Depressurize slowly then remove the lid, carefully remove the pudding, and unmold onto a serving plate.

Meanwhile make the sauce by melting the butter, sugar, and corn syrup together, stirring frequently. Once the sugar has dissolved, slowly stir in the cream, bring to a boil, and boil gently for 2 minutes. Serve with the pudding.

Serves **6**
Cook control **10 lb**
Preparation time **10 minutes**
Presteaming time **15 minutes**
Pressure cooking time
 25 to 30 minutes

FOR THE SPONGE
2 tsp oil
1 stick sweet butter
½ cup dark brown sugar

2 medium eggs, beaten
1 cup self-rising flour
2 Tbsp light corn syrup
1 cup chopped pitted dates
¼ cup pecans, chopped

FOR THE SAUCE
½ stick sweet butter
¼ cup dark brown sugar
2 tbsp light corn syrup
1 cup light cream

ORANGE AND APRICOT
CRÈME BRÛLÉE

IF LIKED YOU CAN VARY THE DRIED FRUIT. TRY DRIED CRANBERRIES OR BLUEBERRIES OR A MIXTURE OF BOTH. FRESH FRUIT CAN ALSO BE USED BUT THESE NEED TO BE FIRM IN TEXTURE SO THAT THEY DO NOT BREAK UP DURING COOKING.

Lightly oil four $^2/_3$-cup ramekin dishes, place the chopped apricots in the bases, and set aside. Heat the cream with the orange zest and orange-flower water to just below boiling point then remove from the heat and reserve.

Whisk the egg yolks with the superfine sugar until creamy then whisk in the cream mixture. Pour over the apricots and cover each dish with a double sheet of waxed paper and secure.

Place the trivet rim-side down into the cooker and pour $1^1/_4$ cups boiling water and the lemon juice into the cooker. Place the ramekins onto the trivet, close the lid, and bring to 15 lb pressure. Cook for 4 minutes then depressurize slowly.

Carefully remove and discard the waxed paper then chill for at least 4 hours.

Sprinkle the tops with the raw brown sugar then place under a preheated broiler and cook, turning the ramekins frequently until the sugar dissolves and caramelizes. Chill again before serving. Garnish with mint sprigs and apricots.

(You may find that four ramekins do not fit inside the cooker. If so, either do in two batches or use mini ramekins.)

Serves **4**
Cook control **15 lb**
Preparation time **5 minutes plus chilling time**
Open cooking time **4 minutes**
Pressure cooking time **4 minutes**

¾ cup dried apricots, chopped
2½ cups whipping cream
1 Tbsp fine grated orange zest
1 Tbsp orange-flower water
4 large egg yolks
1 Tbsp superfine sugar
1 Tbsp lemon juice
¼ cup raw brown sugar

TO GARNISH
Mint sprigs and fresh sliced apricots or extra dried apricots

WHITE BURGUNDY PEARS

CHOOSE FIRM PEARS OF A SIMILAR SIZE AND SHAPE THAT WILL FIT COMFORTABLY INTO THE PRESSURE COOKER. TRY THEM WITH DIFFERENT FLAVORS OF ICE CREAM AS AN ACCOMPANIMENT.

Serves **6**
Cook control **15 lb**
Preparation time **5 minutes**
Open cooking time **3 minutes**
Pressure cooking time **3 minutes**

6 dessert pears
1 small orange
1¼ cups white burgundy wine
6 cloves
2 cinnamon sticks, bruised
¼ cup sugar
2 Tbsp brandy

TO GARNISH
Mint sprigs and extra pared orange zest

TO SERVE
Sweet cookies and vanilla ice cream

Peel the pears as thinly as possible, keeping the stalks intact. Set aside. Pare the zest from the orange and squeeze out the juice.

Place the pears in the cooker with the orange zest, juice, wine, cloves, cinnamon, and sugar. Spoon the wine a few times over the pears then close the lid. Bring to 15 lb pressure and cook for 3 minutes.

Depressurize slowly then remove the lid and lift out the pears. Set aside on a serving dish.

Add the brandy to the liquid in the cooker, bring to a rapid boil, and boil for 3 minutes. Strain over the pears then cool and chill until required.

Decorate with mint sprigs and pared orange zest and serve with cookies and ice cream.

LEMON DRIZZLE PUDDING

WHEN DONE, THIS PUDDING SEPARATES INTO TWO, GIVING A DELICIOUS LEMONY SAUCE ON THE BASE TOPPED WITH A LIGHT FLUFFY SPONGE.

Serves **6**
Cook control **10 lb**
Preparation time **12 minutes**
Presteaming time **15 minutes**
Pressure cooking time
10 minutes

1 stick sweet butter, softened
1 cup superfine sugar
2 medium eggs, beaten
¾ cup self-rising flour
2 Tbsp finely grated lemon zest
2 Tbsp ground almonds
½ tsp baking powder, sifted
4 Tbsp lemon juice
1 Tbsp confectioner's sugar

Lightly oil a 6¼-cup ovenproof dish. Cream the butter with ¼ cup of the superfine sugar until light and fluffy then gradually beat in the eggs a little at a time, adding 2 teaspoons of flour with each addition.

When all the eggs have been added, stir in 1 tablespoon of lemon zest with the remaining flour, the ground almonds, and baking powder. Spoon into the prepared dish.

Mix the remaining sugar, lemon zest, and juice with 1¼ cups of boiling water and pour into the dish. Cover with a double layer of waxed paper with a pleat in the center and secure.

Place the trivet rim-side down in the cooker with an extra 2 tablespoons of lemon juice. Place the dish into the cooker and pour in 4 cups boiling water.

Close the lid and presteam for 15 minutes. Bring to 10 lb pressure and cook for 10 minutes. Depressurize slowly and serve sprinkled with the sifted confectioner's sugar.

DRIED FRUIT COMPOTE

CHOOSE YOUR FAVORITE DRIED FRUIT AND SERVE
WITH PLENTY OF CREAM OR CRÈME FRAÎCHE.

Serves **4 to 6**
Cook control **15 lb**
Preparation time **3 minutes**
   plus 10 minutes soaking time
Pressure cooking time
   10 minutes

4 cups mixed dried fruits
4 to 5 cardamom pods, bruised
¼ cup light brown sugar
2 Tbsp brandy

TO SERVE
Lightly whipped cream or crème
   fraîche and sweet cookies

Place the dried fruit in a large bowl, cover with 4 cups boiling
water and leave for 10 minutes.

Drain, reserving the soaking liquid, and arrange in layers with
the cardamom pods and sugar in the cooker then pour over the
soaking liquid and the brandy. Close the lid and bring to 15 lb
pressure. Cook for 10 minutes then depressurize slowly.

Remove from the cooker and serve warm or chilled with the
cream or crème fraîche and cookies.

BARBECUE RELISH

THIS DELICIOUS RELISH IS IDEAL TO SERVE WITH
MOST MEATS, AND ALSO GOES WELL WITH CHEESE.

Makes **3 pints**
Cook control **10 lb**
Preparation time **15 minutes**
Open cooking time **20 minutes**
Pressure cooking time
   10 minutes

1½ lb tart cooking apples,
   peeled, cored, and chopped
2 lb ripe but firm tomatoes,
   chopped

1 large onion, peeled and
   chopped
4 garlic cloves, peeled and
   crushed
2 to 3 red chiles, seeded and
   chopped
2 tsp whole-grain mustard
2 Tbsp tomato paste
2 cups red wine vinegar
1 cup dark soft brown sugar
2 Tbsp chopped fresh cilantro

Place the cooking apples, tomatoes, onion, garlic, and chiles
into the open cooker then stir in the mustard, tomato paste,
and 1¼ cups vinegar. Stir well then close the lid and bring to
10 lb pressure. Cook for 10 minutes.

Depressurize slowly then stir in the remaining vinegar, the sugar,
and chopped cilantro. Place over a gentle heat and stir until the
sugar has dissolved.

Increase the heat and boil for about 20 minutes or until a thick
consistency is reached. Pot into sterilized warm jars and cover
tightly. Store in the refrigerator up to 3 weeks.

LEMON CURD

FEW THINGS ARE MORE DELICIOUS THAN HOMEMADE LEMON CURD SPREAD ON FRESHLY BAKED BREAD.

Beat the eggs and strain into a bowl that fits easily inside the cooker. Stir in the sugar, lemon zest, and juice. Cut the butter into small pieces and add to the bowl then cover with a double thickness of waxed paper. Secure firmly around the rim with twine.

Pour 2 cups water and a little lemon juice into the cooker with the trivet rim-side down. Put the bowl into the cooker and close the lid.

Bring to 15 lb pressure and cook for 10 minutes. Release the steam slowly. Carefully remove the waxed paper, whisk the lemon curd well (it may have separated a little) until thick and smooth then put into a sterilized warm jar. Cover with a tightly fitting lid and store in the refrigerator up to one week.

Makes **one pint**
Cook control **15 lb**
Preparation time **12 to 15 minutes**
Pressure cooking time **10 minutes**

3 medium eggs
1 cup superfine sugar
Finely grated zest of 2, preferably
   unwaxed, lemons
3 Tbsp lemon juice
½ stick sweet butter

APRICOT CHUTNEY

THIS RECIPE ENABLES YOU NOT ONLY TO USE YOUR OWN HOMEGROWN FRUIT AND VEGETABLES
BUT ALSO TO EXPERIMENT WITH DIFFERENT FLAVORS.

Makes **Four 1-pint jars**

Cook control **15 lb**

Preparation time **10 minutes plus 10 minutes soaking time**

Open cooking time **5 to 10 minutes**

Pressure cooking time **10 minutes**

1 lb dried apricots

1 lb tart cooking apples, peeled, cored, and chopped

1½ cups raisins

1 large onion, peeled and chopped

2 to 3 red chiles, seeded and chopped

2 Tbsp ground ginger

Grated zest and juice 1 lemon

2 cups white wine vinegar

1 cup light brown sugar

Place the apricots in a bowl, cover with boiling water, and soak for 10 minutes. Drain and chop then place in the cooker with the apple, raisins, onion, chiles, ginger, lemon zest, and juice, and 1¼ cups of the vinegar.

Stir well, close the lid, and bring to 15 lb pressure and cook for 10 minutes before releasing the pressure slowly.

Stir in the remaining vinegar and sugar. Boil in the open cooker stirring occasionally for 5 to 10 minutes or until a thick consistency is formed. Put in warm sterilized jars and cover tightly. Store in the refrigerator up to 3 weeks.

MIXED CITRUS MARMALADE

SEVILLE ORANGES ARE WONDERFUL FOR MAKING MARMALADE, BUT THEY HAVE A VERY SHORT SEASON. WHEN THEY ARE UNAVAILABLE, I MAKE THIS MARMALADE, WHICH IS QUITE EASY TO PREPARE AND TASTES DELICIOUS.

Makes **Seven pints**

Cook control **15 lb**

Preparation time **35 minutes**

Open cooking time **15 minutes**

Pressure cooking time **10 minutes**

2 large oranges

1 red grapefruit

2 lemons

8 cups white sugar

1 Tbsp butter

Scrub the fruit, halve it, and squeeze out the juice. Cut the fruit into quarters. Remove the pips and pith from the fruit and place them in a piece of cheesecloth, then tie to secure.

Place all the fruit juice, the fruit quarters, the cheesecloth bag, and 2½ cups water into the cooker and close the lid. Bring to 15 lb pressure and cook for 10 minutes then depressurize quickly.

Remove and discard the cheesecloth bag with the pith and pips. Strain the juice, then return to the cooker. When the fruit quarters are cool enough to handle, shred into thick strips then return to the cooker.

Add the sugar and a further 1¼ cups water then return to the heat and cook, stirring frequently until the sugar has dissolved.

Add the butter then bring to a boil and boil rapidly until setting point is reached. Skim if necessary then pot into warm sterilized jars and cover tightly. Store in the refrigerator up to 1 month.

INDEX

Almond and Pecan-stuffed Chicken
    Breasts 70
Angler Fish, Navarin of, with
    Spring Vegetables 44
Apple & Caraway, Red Cabbage with 97
Apricot Chutney 126—7
Apricot & Cranberry-stuffed Turkey 77
Apricot & Orange Crème Brûlée 121
Asparagus & Bell Pepper Turkey Roulade 86

Barbecue Relish 124
Barbecued Pork Ribs 48—9
Bean Gazpacho 27
Bean Salad with Pecan Dressing 107
beef
    Broth 24
    with Caper Dumplings 57
    Herb Meat Loaf 66
    Olives 62
    in Sour Cream Sauce 56
    Spiced Beef Pot Roast 54
Black-eyed Peas & Chicken Casserole 85
Borscht 27
Boston Baked Beans with Pork 52—3
Brown Rice with Basil 115
bulgur wheat
    Lamb with Eggplant 63
    Pilau 109
Butternut Squash Casserole 90

Cajun Turkey 75
Cannellini Beans & Olive, Rock Cornish
    Hens with 79
Caper Dumplings, Beef with 57
Caribbean Chicken 80
Carrot & Lentil Soup 23
chicken
    & Black-eyed Peas Casserole 85
    Breasts, Almond & Pecan-stuffed 70
    Broth 25
    Caribbean 80
    Chasseur 68
    Cilantro 71
    Coq au Vin 69
    Herb Meat Loaf 66
    Lemon-braised, with Cumin 84
    with Okra & Fennel Tagine 72
    Spiced, with Cranberries & Orange 81
Chile Bean Pot 106
Chocolate Steamed Puddings 118
Coconut-flavored Haddock 37
cod
    Provençal Cod Loin 38
    Spicy Fish Steaks 35
Corn on the Cob with Herb & Garlic
    Butter 93
Couscous, Vegetable 114
Creole Okra Stew 96—7

Dried Fruit Compote 124
Duck with Figs & Port 82
Dumplings, Caper, Beef with 57

eggplant
    Lamb with 63
    Ratatouille 102

Farmhouse Pâté 60—1
Fava Bean & Bacon Succotash 101
Figs & Port, Duck with 82
fish
    Broth 24
    Coconut-flavored Haddock 37
    Navarin of Angler Fish with Spring
        Vegetables 44
    Oriental Sea Bass 42
    Provençal Cod Loin 38
    Salmon with Mushroom Sauce 32
    Smoked Haddock Pilaf 41
    Spinach & Pine Nut-stuffed Sole 34
    Steaks, Spicy 35
    Trout with Herb Butter 39
    Warm Tuna & Pasta Salad 40
Fragrant New Potatoes with Shallots 94

Ginger & Orange Pork 61
Grape Leaves, Stuffed 58
Green Rice 104—5

haddock
    Coconut-flavored 37
    Smoked Haddock Pilaf 41
    Spicy Fish Steaks 35
Herb Meat Loaf 66
Hummus 116

lamb
    with Eggplant 63
    Herb Meat Loaf 66
    Italian, with Pasta 64
    with Pinto Beans 53
    Stuffed Grape Leaves 58
Lemon Curd 125
Lemon Drizzle Pudding 123
Lemon-braised Chicken with Cumin 84
lentils
    Carrot & Lentil Soup 23
    Puy Lentil & Rice Pilaf 112

Maple-glazed Baby Root Vegetables 92—3
Marmalade, Mixed Citrus 127
Meat Loaf, Herb 66
Mexican Pinto Bean Soup 18

okra
    & Fennel Tagine, Chicken with 72
    Stew, Creole 96—7

Olive & Cannellini Beans, Rock Cornish
    Hens with 79
Orange & Apricot Crème Brûlée 121
Orange & Ginger Pork 61
Orange & Prune Stuffing, Pork with 50
Oriental Sea Bass 42

Paprika Pork 51
pasta
    with Fruit & Beans 110
    Italian Lamb with 64
    Spiced 113
    & Tuna Salad, Warm 40
Pears, White Burgundy 122—3
Pesto Soup 26
pine nuts
    Pesto Soup 26
    Spinach & Pine Nut-stuffed Sole 34
Pineapple, Sweet-&-Sour Pork with 46
pinto beans
    Lamb with 53
    Pinto Bean Soup, Mexican 18
pork
    & Apricot Casserole 49
    Boston Baked Beans with 52—3
    Farmhouse Pâté 60—1
    Ginger & Orange 61
    Herb Meat Loaf 66
    Paprika 51
    with Prune & Orange Stuffing 50
    Ribs, Barbecued 48—9
    Sweet-&-Sour, with Pineapple 46
Port & Figs, Duck with 82
Potato & Spinach Vichyssoise 30
potatoes
    Dauphinois 95
    Fragrant New Potatoes with Shallots 94
    Shrimp Chowder 22—3
Prune & Orange Stuffing, Pork with 50

Ratatouille 102
red cabbage
    with Apple & Caraway 97
    Rock Cornish Hens with 78
Relish, Barbecue 124
rice
    Brown, with Basil 115
    Green 104—5
    Oriental Sea Bass 42
    Puy Lentil & Rice Pilaf 112
    Smoked Haddock Pilaf 41
    Stuffed Grape Leaves 58
    Wild Mushroom Risotto 108
Roasted Bell Pepper Soup 29
rock cornish hens
    with Cannellini Beans & Olive 79
    with Kumquats 74
    with Red Cabbage 78

Salmon with Mushroom Sauce 32
Sausage meat, Farmhouse Pâté 60—1
Sea Bass, Oriental 42
Shallots, Fragrant New Potatoes with 94
Shrimp Chowder 22—3
Smoked Haddock Pilaf 41
Sole, Spinach & Pine Nut-stuffed 34
soup
    Bean Gazpacho 27
    Beef Broth 24
    Borscht 27
    Carrot & Lentil 23
    Chicken Broth 25
    Chilled Watercress 20
    Fish Broth 24
    Mexican Pinto Bean 18
    Pesto 26
    Potato & Spinach Vichyssoise 30
    Roasted Bell Pepper 29
    Shrimp Chowder 22—3
    Tomato & Garbanzo 28
    Vegetable Broth 30
    Wild Mushroom 21
Sour Cream Sauce, Beef in 56
Spiced Beef Pot Roast 54
Spiced Pasta 113
Spicy Fish Steaks 35
spinach
    & Pine Nut-stuffed Sole 34
    potato & Spinach Vichyssoise 30
Sticky Toffee Pudding 120
Stuffed Grape Leaves 58
Sweet-&-Sour Pork with Pineapple 46
swordfish
    Spicy Fish Steaks 35

Thai Vegetables 98
Tomato & Garbanzo Soup 28
Trout with Herb Butter 39
Tuna & Pasta Salad, Warm 40
turkey
    Apricot & Cranberry-stuffed 77
    Cajun 75
    Jamaican Spiced 88
    Roulade, Asparagus & Bell Pepper 86
    with Tarragon 71

Vegetable Broth 30
Vegetable Couscous 114

Watercress Soup, Chilled 20
White Burgundy Pears 122—3
Wild Mushroom Risotto 108
Wild Mushroom Soup 21
Winter Vegetable Stew 91